1997

THE MARINER'S BOOK of DAYS

PETER H. SPECTRE

To Ken.
Thanks for everything.

Bob.

Thanks to Jonathan Wilson, Sherry Streeter,
and Kathleen Brandes for their fine work
on the production of this book.

Copyright ©1996 by Peter H. Spectre
Compass Rose, Pleasant Ridge Road, Camden, Maine 04843

Design by Sherry Streeter Design, Brooklin, Maine

Printed in the United States of America

Cover: "On the Deep Sea", oil painting by Walter Dean.
From the collection of the William A. Farnsworth Library
and Art Museum. For further information, write the
Museum at P.O. Box 466, Rockland, Maine 04841.

 A WoodenBoat Book

ISBN: 0-937822-37-X

*Shipmates, if you wish to follow the flood of this fresh
tide, if you seek an anchorage in its eddies, if you long
for a friendly sea-tanged breeze, and desire communion
with the skies, the sea, its little ships, and wish with me
to stand on another long leg to windward, I can promise
you that in books for many years to come new designs
will be born, new words about the sea written — with
now and then a sharp look astern to gather and record
further the charms of times when I was very young . . . .*
—*William Atkin*

The sea is forever quivering,
The shore forever still;
And the boy who is born in a
*   seacoast town*
Is born with a dual will:
The sun-burned rocks and
*   beaches*
Inveigle him to stay;
While every wave that breaches
Is a nudge to be up and away.
                    —Wilbert Snow

PREPARATIONS FOR GETTING UNDERWAY

In a sailboat
- Ensure the sheets are ready to run free, winch handles are at hand, and halyards and downhauls are rigged for immediate use.

In a motorboat or an auxiliary sailboat
- Sound the fuel tank.
- Check that the cooling water is circulating unimpeded.
- Determine the position of the helm, and see that it turns freely.
- Make sure that nothing is foul of the propeller, and that the slack is out of the stern line so it cannot foul the propeller.

In a boat of any type with a compass
- Make sure no loose ferrous metal objects, such as a knife or an iron pot, are near the compass.

THE FIRST BROKER

According to W.P. Stephens, the first yacht broker in the United States was Edward Fox, founder of *Fox's Yachting Annual*, established in 1872. His office was at 83 Nassau Street, New York City.

A FEW THOUGHTS ON YACHT BROKERS AND SURVEYORS

The yacht broker is involved in the sale of the boat, not the determination of its condition.

The surveyor is involved in the determination of the condition of the boat, not its sale.

Never confuse one with the other. Take with a grain of salt the broker's word on the condition of the boat and the surveyor's estimate of the value of the boat.

A conventional yacht broker represents the seller, not the buyer. When push comes to shove, the seller's interest will always come first in the mind and actions of the broker. As a buyer, never fool yourself into thinking otherwise.

A buyer's broker represents the buyer, not the seller. If you engage the services of a buyer's broker, put the agreement in writing.

A surveyor represents the person who hires him. When buying a boat, always hire your own surveyor; do not ask the broker to hire one for you.

Surveyors are paid by fee, usually based on an hourly or daily rate, plus expenses. The fee is payable whether or not the sale goes through.

Yacht brokers are paid by commission as a percentage of the sale price. No sale, no commission. The greater the sale price, the larger the commission.

The yacht broker's commission is paid by the seller, not the buyer.

As a buyer, when in doubt about conflicting reports on the condition of a boat from the broker and the surveyor, take the word of the surveyor.

*The sound of the windlass pawls always thrills me
—it's the sound of getting underway, maybe to far
places, adventure, what the whole thing is about.*
— R.D. "Pete" Culler

DEC/JAN

Monday
30
1956—Dr. Hannes Lindemann, studying the
effects of hardship on shipwrecked sailors,
landed at St. Martin, West Indies, after crossing the Atlantic from Las Palmas, Canary
Islands, in a folding kayak rigged for sail.

Tuesday
31
1840—Herman Melville took a berth as
a common seaman in the whaler *Acushnet*
out of New Bedford, Massachusetts. He
would use much of what he learned
aboard ship in his novel *Moby-Dick*.

Wednesday
1   NEW YEAR'S DAY

1872—The inaugural edition of *Fox's
Yachting Annual*, the first register of
American yachts, was published.

Thursday
2

1932—The first frostbite race, for sailing
dinghies, got underway in Manhasset Bay,
Port Washington, New York.

Friday
3
1885—The brigantine *Mary Celeste* ran
aground on the Rochelais Bank off Haiti and
was wrecked. In 1872, in one of the great
unsolved mysteries, she had been found at
sea, sailing herself, with no one on board.

Saturday
4

1987—Knud Reimers, noted
Scandinavian yacht designer,
died in Sweden.

Sunday
5

1779—Stephen Decatur, future
hero of the U.S. Navy, was born
at Sunnepuxent, Maryland.

HOW TO ACQUIRE A BOAT, IN THE ORDER OF THE LEAST EXPENSIVE TO THE MOST EXPENSIVE METHODS

Buy a used boat.

Build one yourself.

Buy a new, stock boat.

Choose a stock design and have the boat built.

Commission a custom design and have it built.

HOW TO DETERMINE WHICH BOAT IS FOR YOU

Ask around the waterfront.

Read a range of books by a range of authors.

Sail on a variety of boats, owned by a variety of sailors, in a variety of conditions.

Listen to your inner ear, then discount half of what you hear.

HOW *NOT* TO DETERMINE WHICH BOAT IS FOR YOU

Consider the word of the yacht broker as absolute.

Believe the results of a "boat test" published in a popular boating consumer magazine.

Take literally the claims in advertisements.

I should much prefer first to taste a handy little packet by the feel of the helm and the song of wind in her rigging, rather than by the excited and prejudiced comment and predictions of her owner.
— Carl D. Lane

THE DIFFERENCE BETWEEN A USED BOAT IN EXCELLENT CONDITION AND A NEW ONE

Most used boats are sold completely equipped, or nearly so. New boats, in the best of circumstances, are offered with only the barest minimum of necessary equipment. If the price is equal for a new and a used boat, the new one will still cost you more when the docking lines, fire extinguishers, flashlights, electronics, auxiliary bilge pumps, rigging enhancements, towel racks, and the like are figured in.

THE WELL-SEASONED BOAT, ACCORDING TO E.F. KNIGHT

With boats it is as with human beings. Even as a human life is more secure after it has safely passed the period of infantile ailments, so, too, the vessel that has knocked about for years is to be relied on if she still shows no symptoms of decay.

PROFESSOR SPECTRE'S FIVE LEVELS OF ANTIQUE- OR CLASSIC-BOAT BUYING
(highest = 1, lowest = 5)

Level 1—Buy only the best boat with the best provenance.

Level 2—Buy a specific type, or a production boat built by a specific builder.

Level 3—Buy anything as long as it is older than you are and is planked in mahogany.

Level 4—Buy anything as long as it is older than you are.

Level 5—Buy anything.

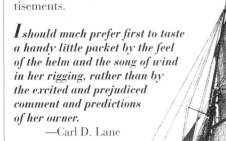

You may think that the equation is "boat and water." It's not. It's "money and boat." The water is not really necessary.
—from *The Shipping News*, E. Annie Proulx

Monday
6

1929—A 50-cent stamp depicting the racing-fishing schooner *Bluenose* was issued by the government of Canada.

Tuesday
7

With a very few exceptions, do not lend your boat to anyone—it never pays.
—L. Francis Herreshoff

Wednesday
8

1609—Henry Hudson signed a contract with the Dutch East India Company to undertake a voyage to the westward to seek a northern route to the East Indies.

Thursday
9

1978—A great storm swept the northeast coast of the United States from Virginia to Maine, causing extreme destruction and coastal flooding.

Friday
10

No surveyor ever says any boat is perfect, certainly not a new one, and certainly not one he has surveyed. —Ian Nicolson

Saturday
11

1911—The first issue of *The Mariner's Mirror*, the British journal of maritime history, was published.

Sunday
12

1779—A standard marine insurance policy form, the first of its kind, was adopted by Lloyd's of London, largest association of underwriters in the world.

The Earl of Balcarres, East Indiaman

THE "LOOK" OF SHIPS, ACCORDING TO DAVID W. BONE

Fashion, as it is understood in dress and national costume, has its counterpart in the structure of ships, and, like dress, this variety in design—indicative of local and national character—is largely brought about by climate and the associations of the routes on which the vessels ply.

REST ASSURED WHEN READING KIPLING, SAYS WILLIAM MCFEE, NOVELIST AND MARINE ENGINEER

One of our eminent literary critics, who was writing a book on Kipling, but who had no knowledge of ships or machinery, once inquired of me if all that technical stuff in Kipling's stories had any real accuracy. It was a pleasure to reassure that eminent critic. To my knowledge Kipling never made a mistake. Some of his detail, when one remembers he was a journalist by profession, was clairvoyant.

FROM *CAPTAINS COURAGEOUS*, BY RUDYARD KIPLING

She might have been the very *Flying Dutchman*, so foul, draggled, and unkempt was every rope and stick aboard. Her old-style quarter-deck was some four or five feet high, and her rigging flew knotted and tangled like weed at a wharf-end. She was running before the wind—yawing frightfully—her staysail let down to act as a sort of extra foresail,—"scandalised," they call it,—and her foreboom guyed out over the side. Her bowsprit cocked up like an old-fashioned frigate's; her jib-boom had been fished and spliced and nailed and clamped beyond further repair; and as she hove herself forward, and sat down on her broad tail, she looked for all the world like a blowzy, frowzy, bad old woman sneering at a decent girl.

Heh! Tally on! Aft and walk away with her!
Handsome to the cathead, now; O tally on the fall!
Stop, seize and fish, and easy on the davit guy.
Up, well up the fluke of her, and inboard haul!

Well, ah fare you well, for the Channel wind took hold of us,
Choking down our voices as we snatch the gaskets free.
And it's blowing up for night,
And she's dropping Light for Light,
And she's snorting under bonnets for a breath of open sea.
—from "Anchor Song," by Rudyard Kipling

VARYING DEFINITIONS OF THE TONNAGE OF A SHIP

Displacement tonnage—the weight of water displaced by the hull when it is floating at its load waterline

Deadweight tonnage—the total weight of cargo and stores a vessel is capable of carrying when floating at its load waterline

Gross tonnage—the total internal volume of a vessel; 100 cubic feet is considered to be equal to one ton

Net tonnage—the internal volume of a vessel available for cargo; the gross tonnage minus engine and bunker spaces, crew quarters, navigational areas, etc.; 100 cubic feet is considered to be equal to one ton

'Twas them days a ship was part of the sea,
and a man was part of the ship, and the sea
joined all together and made it one.
—from *The Hairy Ape*, by Eugene O'Neill

JANUARY

Monday
13

1835—The brig *Pilgrim*, aboard which
Richard Henry Dana, Jr., sailed before
the mast, arrived off Santa Barbara,
California, 150 days out from Boston.

Tuesday
14

*We should all be the fitter, the happier and
better if we could return to the wide hori-
zons of land and sea.* —Basil Lubbock

Wednesday
15

1951—The U.S. government completed a two-week sale of 131 surplus
World War II ships—91 Liberty cargo,
10 Liberty tanker, 20 Victory cargo,
and 10 C-4 cargo ships.

Thursday
16

1962—S.S. (Samuel Supplee) Rabl,
small-craft designer and author of
Boatbuilding in Your Own Backyard,
died in Baltimore, Maryland.

Friday
17

1912—Robert Falcon Scott and four
companions reached the South Pole,
only to find that a Norwegian expedition under Roald Amundsen had
preceded them by a month.

Saturday
18

1936—Rudyard Kipling, author of
Captains Courageous and winner of
the 1907 Nobel Prize for Literature,
died in London, England.

Sunday
19

1935—The Gloucester fishing
schooner *Elsie*, loser in 1921 to the
Lunenburger *Bluenose* at the second
International Fishermen's Races, sank
in the Gulf of St. Lawrence.

AN ACT TO CREATE THE COAST GUARD

There shall be established in lieu of the existing Revenue-Cutter Service and the Life-Saving Service, to be composed of those two organizations, the Coast Guard, which shall constitute a part of the military forces of the United States and which shall operate under the Treasury Department in time of peace and operate as a part of the Navy, subject to the orders of the Secretary of the Navy, in time of war or when the President shall so direct.

THE COAST GUARD CUTTER

But the men that sail the ocean
In a wormy, rotten craft,
When the sea ahead is mountains
With a hell-blown gale abaft;
When the mainmast cracks and topples,
And she's lurching in the trough,
Them's the guys that greets the cutter
With the smiles that won't come off.
　　　　　　—Arthur Somers Roche

A FEW OF THE YACHT DESIGNERS WHO CUT THEIR TEETH IN THE DESIGN OFFICE OF JOHN ALDEN

Carl Alberg
Howard I. Chapelle
S.S. Crocker
Charles MacGregor
William McNary
Al Mason
K. Aage Nielsen
Murray Peterson
Charles Schock
Clifford Swaine
Winthrop L. Warner
Fenwick Williams
Ralph Winslow
Charles W. Wittholz

HOW LONG IS SHE?

Length overall—extreme measurement; from the foremost to the aftermost part of the vessel, including everything

Length on the waterline—foremost to aftermost of the waterline when the vessel is loaded normally

Length on deck—foremost to aftermost of the main deck

Length between perpendiculars—measured between the forward part of the stem and the after part of the rudderpost

HOW WIDE IS SHE?

Beam—the maximum width of the vessel, not including fittings and rubrails

Extreme beam—the maximum width of the vessel, including fittings and rubrails

Beam at the waterline—the maximum width of the vessel at the waterline plane

Beam amidships—the width of the vessel measured midway between the ends

HOW DEEP IS SHE?

Depth—the vertical measurement from the bottom of the keel to the sheerline

Molded depth—the vertical measurement from the deck to the top of the keel

Draft—the vertical measurement from the designed waterline to the lowermost edge of the keel

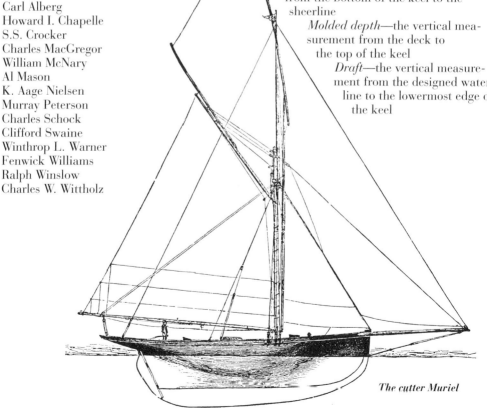

The cutter Muriel

[Coastguardsmen] will always keep in mind that their countrymen are freemen, and, as such, are impatient of everything that bears the least mark of domineering spirit. —Alexander Hamilton

Monday
20   MARTIN LUTHER KING'S BIRTHDAY

1915—The Revenue-Cutter Service and the Life-Saving Service were combined to create a new armed service, the United States Coast Guard.

Tuesday
21

1877—The down-easter *Grandee*, in the Southern Ocean on a passage to Melbourne, ran head-on into an iceberg and survived, one of the few wooden ships to do so.

Wednesday
22

1920—The Greek schooner *Gortynia*, ex-*George H. Ames*, abandoned at sea, was towed into Bermuda bottom up.

Thursday ◯
23

1946—Lieutenant Commander Joseph T. O'Callahan became the first chaplain in the U.S. Navy to be awarded the Congressional Medal of Honor.

Friday
24

1884—Yacht designer John Alden was born in Troy, New York.

Saturday
25

1841—Admiral John "Jackie" Fisher, First Sea Lord of the British Royal Navy in the years preceding World War I, was born in Rambodde, Ceylon.

Sunday
26

1949—The USS *Norton Sound* became the first ship of the U.S. Navy to launch a guided missile.

THE ACCOMMODATION PIPE DREAM, ACCORDING TO MAURICE GRIFFITHS

Nearly all beginners plan far too much accommodation for the dimensions of the boat they have in mind. Sketched on the backs of old envelopes or on the menu at the lunch table our early dreams show plans for the layout below decks that could never be fitted inside the hull.

For myself, I would sooner live in squalid comfort than be miserable in bad weather.
—R.D. "Pete" Culler

WHEN A LOT IS TOO MUCH

In some circumstances, accommodations that are too generous can be a disadvantage. An extra-wide berth can be a luxury when at anchor in a snug harbor; at sea in a gale, it can be too wide for you to wedge yourself in securely. So, too, an open-plan galley—room to roam at anchor; no surfaces against which to brace yourself when being tossed around by high seas.

THE FORECASTLE OF A TYPICAL NORTH AMERICAN DEEPWATER MERCHANT SAILING SHIP IN THE 1830S, ACCORDING TO W.S. LINDSAY, WHO SERVED HIS APPRENTICESHIP IN ONE

At all times it was a foulsome and suffocating abode, and in bad weather the water and filth that washed about the deck, and among the chests and casks, created the most intolerable and loathsome stench.

Here, however, these fourteen sailors and apprentices slept, washed, dressed, and had their food, except in fine weather, when they took their meals on deck, their food consisting almost entirely of inferior salted pork, beef which was sometimes nearly as hard and unpalatable as the kids in which it was served, and brown biscuits too often mouldy and full of maggots. To make matters worse, the forecastle of the ship was full of rats, and I have the most vivid recollection of one of these animals on more than one occasion finding its way into the hammock where I slept.

ACCOMMODATIONS DIMENSIONS RECOMMENDED BY S.S. RABL

Standing headroom—6 feet 3 inches
Minimum headroom—at least 4 feet
Sitting headroom over a seat—3 feet from the top of the cushion
Height of seat from floor to top of cushion—maximum 19 inches, normal 16 inches, minimum 12 inches
Width of seat—minimum 12 inches, normal 16 inches
Berth—normal 6 feet 6 inches long, 2 feet 6 inches wide; minimum 6 feet long, 1 foot 9 inches wide

THE BOOKS OF HOWARD I. CHAPELLE

The Baltimore Clipper, 1930
The History of American Sailing Ships, 1935
Yacht Designing and Planning, 1935
Boatbuilding, 1941
The History of the American Sailing Navy, 1949
American Small Sailing Craft, 1951
The National Watercraft Collection, 1960
The Bark Canoes and Skin Boats of North America (with Edwin Tappan Adney), 1964
The Search for Speed Under Sail, 1967
The Constellation Question, 1970
The American Fishing Schooners, 1973

Lead, log, lookout, and be steady.
Keep an eye on the glass, and for changes be ready.
　　　　　　　　　　　　　—anon.

JAN/FEB

Monday
27
1926—In the culmination of a four-days-running rescue, the crew of the U.S. freighter *President Roosevelt*, directed by Captain Robert B. Miller, saved the entire crew of the British freighter *Antinoe*.

Tuesday
28
1915—The four-masted bark *William P. Frye*—the last built by Arthur Sewall of Bath, Maine—became the first American vessel sunk by the Germans in World War I.

Wednesday
29
The inevitable day arrived when I finally gave voice to this confounding madness by screaming, "I've got to get a boat."
　　　　　　　　　　　—Tom McGrath

Thursday
30
1860—During a terrific storm, a rogue wave tore the bell from the Bishop Rock lighthouse off the southwest coast of England. Weighing 300 pounds, the bell was mounted 100 feet up in the tower.

Friday
31
1872—The famed tea clipper *Ariel*, winner of the "Great Tea Race" of 1866, departed London for Sydney, Australia. She never arrived.

Saturday
1
1901—Howard Irving Chapelle, naval architect and maritime historian, was born in Tolland, Massachusetts.

Sunday
2
1921—Antonio Jacobsen, marine artist best known for his ship portraiture, died in West Hoboken, New Jersey.

THE *LONDON CHRONICLE* COMMENTS ON THE *BEDFORD*, THE FIRST AMERICAN SHIP TO TRADE WITH BRITAIN FOLLOWING THE REVOLUTIONARY WAR, AND THE NEW COUNTRY FROM WHICH SHE CAME

There is a vessel in the harbor with a very strange flag. Thirteen is a number peculiar to rebels. A party of prisoners, lately returned from Jersey, says the rations among the rebels are thirteen dried clams a day. Sachem Schuyler has a topknot of thirteen stiff hairs which erect themselves on the crown of his head when he gets mad. It takes thirteen paper dollars to make one shilling. Every well-organized household has thirteen children, all of whom expect to be Major Generals or members of the high and mighty Congress of the thirteen United States when they attain the age of thirteen years. Mrs. Washington has a tomcat with thirteen yellow rings around its tail. His flaunting tail suggested to Congress the same number of stripes for the Rebel Flag.

A FEW WORDS FROM THE LAND OF THE FREE AND THE BRAVE

One of the *Bedford*'s crew was a hunchback. An English sailor, on meeting him, is said to have struck him hard on the hunch and said, "Hello, Jack! What have you got there?"

"Bunker Hill," the American said, "and be damned to you."

CHARACTER, ABOVE ALL, SAYS BASIL LUBBOCK

No cleverness of brain or dexterity of finger can make a great painter or musician, and it is the same when you come to deal with the ship and the horse. Whether you are handling a fiddle or the tiller, a bridle or a paint brush, you need certain almost indefinable qualities of character to be really successful; and if you lack these qualities you remain a piano thumper, a paint dauber, a wrecker of ships and a spoiler of horses.

Come, all you fair maidens in country and town,
Lend your attention to what is pen'd down;
And let your opinions with mine both agree,
Of all sorts of tradesmen a Seaman for me.
　　　　—from "The Seaman's Renown,"
　　　　　　by T. Lanfiere

THE SEAMAN OF TODAY, ACCORDING TO WILLIAM MCFEE

With his daily newspaper and radio entertainment, his fresh provisions and comfortable quarters, his library of books and his short waking hours, his feeling of economic solidarity with all other seafaring men in the world, his voyages so short by comparison that he is never aware of the solitude that was the blessing—or the curse—of sea life in the old days, the seaman of today has more ideological identity with the operator of a truck or train than with the Ancient Mariner and Captain Ahab.

He [the sailor] is an Otter, an Amphibian that lives both on Land and Water.
　　　　—Richard Braithwaite, 1631

Monday
3

Fit out early and lay up late, for life, alas! is brief. —Capt. A.J. Kenealy

Tuesday
4
1991—A rare 1906 Acme Patented Stuffing Box brought the highest price ever, $14,750, to the Wood Neck Marine Antiques Exchange, Sippewissett, Massachusetts, for a marine artifact sold at auction.

Wednesday
5
1783—The ship *Bedford*, Captain Mooers of Nantucket, the first U.S. merchant vessel to trade with Britain following the American Revolutionary War, came to anchor in the River Thames, England.

Thursday
6
1933—The USS *Ramapo*, en route across the Pacific from Manila to San Diego, encountered during a seven-day storm a giant wave estimated to have been 112 feet from trough to crest.

Friday
7
1899—The Electric Boat Company, famed for its submarines and World War II PT boats, was incorporated.

Saturday
8

The small will of the boat must resist the great force of the sea. —James Wharram

Sunday
9
1965—Photographer Albert Cook Church, chronicler of the New England fishing and whaling fleets, died in New Bedford, Massachusetts.

Given enough time, an amateur can build anything.
— Bob Hicks

THINK ABOUT IT

The most important milestone in the progress of wooden boat building was the development of the iron adze. Without it, the boatbuilder might as well have been working with one hand tied behind his back. With it, a skilled shipwright could fashion any part of the structure of a vessel.

TABLET ERECTED ON THE ISLAND OF JUAN FERNANDEZ

In Memory
of
Alexander Selkirk
Mariner

A native of Largo, in the county of Fife, Scotland, who lived on this island in complete solitude for four years and four months. He was landed from the *Cinque Ports* galley, 96 tons, 18 guns, A.D. 1704, and was taken off in the *Duke*, privateer, 12th February 1709. He died Lieutenant of H.M.S. *Weymouth*, A.D. 1723 [actually 1721], aged 47. This tablet is erected near Selkirk's lookout, by Commodore Powell and the officers of H.M.S. *Topaz*, A.D. 1868.

ROBINSON CRUSOE BUILDS A BOAT

I went to work on this boat the most like a fool that ever man did, who had any of his senses awake.... I felled a cedar tree, and I question much whether Solomon ever had such a one for the building of the Temple of Jerusalem; it was five feet ten inches diameter at the lower part next the stump, and four feet eleven inches diameter at the head of twenty-two feet; after which it lessened for a while, and then parted into branches. It was not without infinite labour that I felled this tree; I was twenty days hacking and hewing at it at the bottom; I was fourteen more getting the branches and limbs, and the vast spreading head cut off, which I hacked and hewed through with axe and hatchet, and inexpressible labour: after this, it cost me a month to shape it and dub it to a proportion, and to something like the bottom of a boat, that it might swim upright as it ought to do. It cost me near three months more to clear the inside, and work it out so as to make an exact boat of it; this I did, indeed, without fire, by mere mallet and chisel, and by the dint of hard labour, till I had brought it to be a very handsome periagua, and big enough to have carried six and twenty men, and consequently big enough to have carried me and my cargo.
—from *Robinson Crusoe*, by Daniel Defoe

I wish I was a bosun bold,
Or even a bombardier,
I'd build a boat and away I'd float
And straight to the ocean steer.

And straight to the ocean steer, my boys
Where the dancing dolphins play;
And the whales and sharks are having their
larks
Ten thousand miles away.
—old song

Monday
10

1722—Captain Bartholomew "Black Bart" Roberts, the celebrated pirate, was killed in a battle with HMS *Swallow* off the west coast of Africa.

Tuesday
11

1904—The down-easter *Henry B. Hyde*, considered the finest American full-rigged ship since the clippers, drove ashore on a Virginia beach during a storm and became a total loss.

Wednesday
12 LINCOLN'S BIRTHDAY

1709—Alexander Selkirk, marooned on one of Chile's Juan Fernandez islands since 1704, was rescued by the privateer Duke. Daniel Defoe later based his novel *Robinson Crusoe* on Selkirk's experiences.

Thursday
13

1891—Admiral David Dixon Porter, American Civil War naval hero and author of the *History of the Navy in the War of Rebellion*, died.

Friday
14 ST. VALENTINE'S DAY

1951—The American ship *Bethore*, off the coast of Ecuador, passed a great shoal, approximately 10 miles long, of red crabs swimming just below the surface of the sea.

Saturday
15

1897—The U.S. battleship *Maine* exploded and sank in Havana Harbor, Cuba; the incident contributed to the outbreak of the Spanish-American War.

Sunday
16

1700—HMS *Advice* departed Boston, Massachusetts, carrying Captain William Kidd under guard to London for trial as a pirate.

A MOMENTOUS DEPARTURE, FROM A DESCRIPTION IN THE *MARYLAND JOURNAL* AND *BALTIMORE ADVERTISER*

On Sunday last sailed from New York, the ship *Empress of China*, Captain John Green of this port [New York] for Canton in China. On passing the Garrison at Fort George, she fired with great regularity, the United States salute which was returned from the fort. This handsome, commodious and elegant ship modelled after and built on the new invented construction of the ingenious Mr. Peck, of Boston, is deemed an exceeding swift sailor. The Captain and crew, with several young American adventurers, were all happy and cheerful, in good health and high spirits; and with a becoming decency, elated on being considered the first instruments, in the hands of Providence, who have undertaken to extend the commerce of the United States of America to that distant, and to us, unexplored country.

THE "TRIANGLE" TRADE OF THE 18TH CENTURY

- Rum, money, trading goods to West Africa
- Slaves, gold dust, pepper to the Caribbean
- Sugar, molasses, tropical hardwoods to North America

STOWAGE OF CARGO IN OCEANGOING VESSELS, ROUGHLY SPEAKING

Heavy weights should be distributed along the length of the vessel.

Very heavy weights should be stowed in the middle third, fore and aft, not in the ends.

Two-thirds of the total weight should be in the lower holds, one-third in the 'tween-decks.

Very heavy weights should be stowed in the lower holds, not the 'tween-decks.

OLD TERMINOLOGY FOR LIQUIDCONTAINERS AT SEA (in British imperial measure)

Tank, 400 gallons
Butt, 110 gallons
Puncheon, 72 gallons
Hogshead, 54 gallons
Barrel, 36 gallons
Kilderkin, 18 gallons

It is somewhat of a paradox that the greater the ship, the less cargo she can carry.
—David W. Bone

BOOKKEEPING IN THE OLD MERCHANT MARINE, ACCORDING TO MERCHANT SHIPOWNER WILLIAM GRAY OF BOSTON, 1809

A good captain will sail with a load of fish to the West Indies, hang up a stocking in the cabin on arriving, put therein hard dollars as he sells fish, and pay out when he buys rum, molasses, and sugar, and hand in the stocking on his return full of all accounts.

FLOATING STUFF

Flotsam—wreckage and cargo from a wreck floating on the ocean

Jetsam—cargo deliberately thrown overboard from a vessel, usually to lighten ship in an emergency

Jettison—to throw cargo overboard into the sea

Lagan—cargo thrown overboard and marked with a buoy for later recovery

Wreck—a vessel, or parts of a vessel, or cargo thrown overboard that has washed ashore

The Lord gave us two ends to use: one to think with and one to sit with. The war [World War II] depends on which we choose—heads we win, tails we lose. —**Admiral Chester W. Nimitz, USN**

Monday

17 WASHINGTON'S BIRTHDAY

1755—Commodore Thomas Truxton, one of the original six captains commissioned in the U.S. Navy and first commander of the frigate *Constellation*, was born on Long Island, New York

Tuesday

18

1846—The U.S. Navy officially mandated the words *port* and *starboard* for *left* and *right*; the previously accepted terms were *larboard* and *starboard*.

Wednesday

19

1919—After eight days of grueling competition, Anstead Willey, Jr., took the grand prize at the first annual Lincoln Memorial Time Trials of the Eastern States Quick-Draw Yacht-Design Competition, Sonny's Wharfside, Portland, Maine.

Thursday

20

1966—Admiral Chester W. Nimitz, hero of the Pacific during World War II and the last of the U.S. Navy's five-star fleet admirals, died.

Friday

21

1849—A design for a U.S. yacht ensign, which had been developed by the New York Yacht Club, was approved by the Secretary of the Navy.

Saturday ◯

22

1784—The *Empress of China* departed New York on the first American commercial voyage to China.

Sunday

23

According to sailors, everything on board a ship has a heart.
—George Biddlecombe

THE DIFFERENCE BETWEEN THE STAND OF THE TIDE AND SLACK WATER

Stand of the tide—the period when there is no vertical motion of the tide; the tide is at the top of high water or the bottom of low water.

Slack water—the period when there is no horizontal motion of the water; the tidal current is running neither in nor out.

FACTORS AFFECTING THE HEIGHT OF TIDE COMPUTED FROM TABLES

Strong onshore winds (blowing from the sea toward the land) and a low barometer reading tend to increase the height of high water.

Strong offshore winds (blowing from the land toward the sea) and a high barometer reading tend to decrease the height of high water.

WIND AND TIDE

Lee tide—the wind blows and the tide runs in the same direction.

Weather tide—the wind blows and the tide runs in opposite directions.

MY LOST YOUTH
by Henry Wadsworth Longfellow

Often I think of the beautiful town
*   That is seated by the sea;*
Often in thought go up and down
The pleasant streets of that dear old town,
*   And my youth comes back to me.*
*   And a verse of a Lapland song*
*   Is haunting my memory still:*
"A boy's will is the wind's will,
And the thoughts of youth are long, long
*   thoughts.*

I can see the shadowy lines of its trees,
*   And catch, in sudden gleams,*
The sheen of the far-surrounding seas,
And islands that were the Hesperides
*   Of all my boyish dreams.*
*   And the burden of that old song,*
*   It murmurs and whispers still:*
"A boy's will is the wind's will,
And the thoughts of youth are long, long
*   thoughts."*

I remember the black wharves and the slips,
*   And the sea-tides tossing free;*
And Spanish sailors with bearded lips,
And the beauty and mystery of the ships,

And the magic of the sea.
*   And the voice of that wayward song*
*   Is singing and saying still:*
"A boy's will is the wind's will,
And the thoughts of youth are long, long
*   thoughts."*

I remember the bulwarks by the shore,
*   And the fort upon the hill;*
The sunrise gun, with its hollow roar
The drum-beat repeated o'er and o'er,
*   And the bugle wild and shrill.*
*   And the music of that old song*
*   Throbs in my memory still:*
"A boy's will is the wind's will,
And the thoughts of youth are long, long
*   thoughts."*

I remember the sea-fight far away,
*   How it thundered o'er the tide!*
And the dead captains, as they lay
In their graves, o'erlooking the tranquil bay,
*   Where they in battle died.*
*   And the sound of that mournful song*
*   Goes through me with a thrill:*
"A boy's will is the wind's will,
And the thoughts of youth are long, long
*   thoughts."*

"Wouldst thou," so the helmsman answered,
"Learn the secret of the sea?"
—Henry Wadsworth Longfellow

FEB/MAR

Monday
24

1885—The down-easter *Henry B. Hyde*, arguably
the finest and fastest American-built full-rigged
ship since the clippers, began her maiden voyage
from New York bound for San Francisco.

Tuesday
25

1873—Arthur John Trevor Briscoe, marine
artist, was born in Birkenhead, England.

Wednesday
26

1944—Sue Sophia Dauser became
the first woman to achieve the rank
of captain in the U.S. Navy.

Thursday
27

1807—Henry Wadsworth Longfellow,
author of "The Building of the Ship,"
"The Wreck of the *Hesperus*," "My
Lost Youth," and other poems of the
sea, was born in Portland, Maine.

Friday
28

It is as hard to describe the fascination
of the sea as to explain the beauty of
a woman. —Claud Worth

Saturday
1

Much of the world's history
has been written on the
oceans. —Peter Kemp

Sunday
2

1864—The clipper ship *Snow Squall*
limped into Port Stanley, Falkland Islands,
after being disabled off Tierra del Fuego.
Her hull, the last surviving American
clipper, became part of a jetty.

ON BECOMING A BOATBUILDER, ACCORDING TO DAVID C. "BUD" McINTOSH

There's no mystery to boatbuilding. Anybody can do it: an expert can do it quicker and better, but all you need is some confidence and a little direction and reasonable facility with your hands.

ON BECOMING A BOATBUILDER, ACCORDING TO CARROLL LOWELL

I think you have to be knocked down, beat around, go broke, starve a bit, come up fighting. That's the only way you can be a boatbuilder.

THE GENESIS OF A BOATBUILDING BOOK

In the Fall of 1945 I was visiting the office of Cornell Maritime Press in reference to some other matters when Felix [Cornell] looked across the desk at me and said, "Sam, how about doing a boatbuilding book for us?"...."O.K., Felix, I will"—just like that.

The Spring of 1946 rolled around and I was idly gazing out of the window dreaming of the time when the white perch would start biting down on the bar when the telephone rang. It was a long distance call from New York and Felix was at the other end of the line. "When am I gonna get my book?" he pleaded. "Aw hell, Felix," I entreated, "ya know dam well that I gotta fix up my boat and I wanna build another. Besides this time the fish are starting to bite, and you know I never write when fish are biting."

"T'hell with that," said Felix and added other persuasive language that only those who know Felix can appreciate. In the end Felix won.
—S.S. Rabl

MEMORABLE BOOKS ON WOODEN BOAT BUILDING

Canoe and Boat Building for Amateurs, by W.P. Stephens, Forest and Stream, 1885

Boat Building Simplified, by Herbert J. Ashcroft, Thomas Reed Publishers, 1936

Amateur Boatbuilding, by William F. Crosby, The Rudder Publishing Co., 1938

Boatbuilding, by Howard I. Chapelle, W.W. Norton, 1941

Boatbuilding in Your Own Backyard, by S.S. Rabl, Cornell Maritime Press, 1947

Amateur Boat Building, by Michael Verney, Macmillan & Co., 1948

Small Boat Construction, by Robert M. Steward, The Rudder Publishing Co., 1950 (now published as *Boatbuilding Manual*, International Marine Publishing Co.)

Boat Carpentry, by Hervey Garrett Smith, Van Nostrand Reinhold, 1955

Clenched Lap or Clinker, by Eric McKee, National Maritime Museum, 1972

Boatbuilding Down East, by Royal Lowell, International Marine Publishing Co., 1977

Building Classic Small Craft, by John Gardner, International Marine Publishing Co., 1977

Lapstrake Boatbuilding, by Walter J. Simmons, International Marine Publishing Co., 1978

Instant Boats, by H.H. Payson, International Marine Publishing Co., 1979

How to Build a Wooden Boat, by David C. McIntosh, WoodenBoat Publications, 1987

A corinthian sailor is one capable of managing a craft either single-handed (if she is small enough) or with the assistance of other amateurs.
— Frank Cowper

MARCH

Monday
3

1899—Wireless telegraphy was used for the first time in rendering assistance at sea when the steamship *R.F. Mathews* ran down the East Goodwin Lightship, England.

Tuesday
4

1858—The keel was laid in Toulon, France, for the first oceangoing ironclad warship, the French Navy's frigate *La Gloire*.

Wednesday
5

1932—Arthur D. Story, builder of many of the greatest Gloucester fishing schooners, died in Essex, Massachusetts. Among his credits were the *Carrie Phillips, Elsie, Henry Ford, Columbia*, and *Gertrude L. Thebaud*.

Thursday
6

1874—In honor of its dedication to amateur competition, the Seawanhaka Yacht Club of Oyster Bay, New York, changed its name to the Seawanhaka Corinthian Yacht Club.

Friday
7

The nautical world owes much to those men who possessed both the will and the ability to set down what they knew for future generations. —W.P. Stephens

Saturday
8

1824—The packet *Emerald* arrived in Boston, Massachusetts, after a record passage for a commercial sailing vessel of 15 days, 14 hours, from Liverpool, England.

Sunday
9

1798—George Balfour was appointed the first surgeon in the U.S. Navy.

TYPES OF BALLAST
Inside—the ballast is inside the skin of the boat.

Outside—the ballast is hung from the keel, outside the skin of the boat.

Fixed—the ballast is permanently secured in place.

Shifting—the ballast can be moved according to conditions (in a small craft, the crew, in effect, is shifting ballast).

THE ART OF BALLASTING
The whole art of ballasting consists in placing the center of gravity to correspond with the trim and shape of the vessel, so as neither to be too high nor too low; neither too far forward, nor too far aft; and to lade the ship so deep, that the surface of the water may nearly rise to the extreme breadth amidships; and thus she will be enabled to carry a good sail, incline but little, and ply well to windward.

—William Falconer, *Universal Dictionary of the Marine*, 1769

THE TWO COMPONENTS OF SAILING-YACHT STABILITY
1. That achieved by weight
2. That achieved by the shape of the hull

THE PRICE OF BALLAST, ACCORDING TO ARTHUR BEISER
The stability of a monohull comes partly from her beam and partly from her ballast. Heel her over as far as you like, even turn her upside down, and she will always right herself. The price of this ultimate stability is that such a boat has to lug around a third to a half of her displacement in the form of ballast, the lower down the better.

THE FOUR PURPOSES OF THE SAILING-BOAT KEEL, ACCORDING TO DOUGLAS PHILLIPS-BIRT
1. To produce the hydrofoil action required to resist the lateral component of the wind force
2. To influence steering and handling
3. To provide accommodation and lever for the ballast
4. To support the boat when aground

The more metal we cram into a yacht's intestines, the more we destroy her elasticity and buoyancy in a seaway.
—Vanderdecken

We deal in lead.
—Steve McQueen, *The Magnificent Seven*

BALLASTING MATERIALS
- Lead
- Cast iron
- Fabricated steel
- Reinforced concrete

TRIMMING A SMALL SAILBOAT
When distributing ballast, keep in mind that the crew usually is concentrated aft and its weight will have an effect on trim. To account for this, ballast the boat so it is down slightly by the head without the crew on board.

I wanted to go around Cape Horn in a sailing ship; it was one of the few ambitions in my life that I pursued until I attained it. —Harry Dring

MARCH

Monday
10

1919—Harry Dring, merchant seaman and former keeper of the historic ships at the San Francisco Maritime Museum, was born in Oakland, California.

Tuesday
11

1902—The knockabout *Helen B. Thomas,* the first Gloucester fishing schooner without a bowsprit, was launched in Essex, Massachusetts.

Wednesday
12

1818—Rear Admiral John L. Worden, commander of the U.S. ironclad *Monitor* in her battle with the Confederate ironclad *Merrimac,* was born in Mount Pleasant, New York.

Thursday
13

1896—The compromise cutter *Waxwing,* newly launched and undergoing sea trials off Quisset, Massachusetts, lost her lead ballast keel, rolled over, and sank. Her crew was rescued by a passing fisherman.

Friday
14

1854—The clipper ship *Comet* arrived in New York after a record passage for commercial sailing vessels of 76 days, 7 hours, from San Francisco.

Saturday
15

1809—The "long embargo," created by the U.S. Embargo Act of 1807, ended. American vessels were once again free to clear for and trade with foreign ports.

Sunday
16

1952—A record 73.62 inches of rain fell in a 24-hour period on the island of Reunion, near Madagascar, in the Indian Ocean.

BERNARD MOITESSIER DISCOVERS THE DREAM ISN'T WINNING THE RACE BUT CONTINUING THE DREAM

Of course I will continue toward the Pacific. I can't remember who it was who said, "There are two terrible things for a man: not to have fulfilled his dream, and to have fulfilled it."

Maybe I will be able to go beyond my dream, to get inside of it, where the true thing is, the only real precious fur, the one that keeps you warm forever. Find it, or perhaps never return.

THE CONSTITUENTS OF THE AVERAGE SAMPLE OF SEAWATER

Chloride	55.04%
Sodium	30.61%
Sulfate	7.69%
Magnesium	3.69%
Calcium	1.16%
Potassium	1.10%
Bicarbonate	0.41%
Bromide	0.19%
Boric acid	0.07%
Strontium	0.04%
Fluoride	0.003%
Trace elements	0.01%

THE SACRED COD, MUCH BETTER THAN GOLD

The Coast aboundeth with such multitudes of Codd that the inhabitants of New England doe dung their ground with Codd; and it is a commodity better than the golden mines of the Spanish Indies; for without dried Codd, the Spaniard, Portugal and Italian would not be able to vittel a ship for the Sea.

—Thomas Morton,
New English Canaan, 1632

I will go back to the great sweet mother,
  Mother and lover of men, the sea.
I will go down to her, I and none other,
  Close with her, kiss her and mix her with
  me;
Cling to her, strive with her, hold her fast;
O fair white mother, in days long past
Born without sister, born without brother,
  Set free my soul as thy soul is free.

—from *The Return*,
Algernon Charles Swinburne

THE ZONES OF THE OCEAN

Epipelagic—surface to 650 feet depth, the zone of light penetration

Mesopelagic—650 feet to 6,500 feet, the zone of twilight

Bathypelagic—6,500 feet to 21,000 feet, the zone of darkness

Abyssopelagic—21,000 feet and lower, the zone of blackness

PERHAPS

Perhaps, as I idle away the autumn in the dim beauty of the Essex fenland, and as we drive in the pony-cart through the lanes, we shall stop and the children will say, "If you stand up, you can see the sea."

Perhaps. Who knows?
—William McFee

And goodly Odysseus rejoiced as he set his sails to the breeze. —Homer

I am continuing non-stop towards the Pacific Islands because I am happy at sea, and perhaps also to save my soul. — Bernard Moitessier, in a cable to the *Sunday Times*

MARCH

Monday
17
1784—The Commonwealth of Massachusetts House of Representatives voted to hang a "representation of a cod-fish in the room where the House sit [sic], as a memorial to the importance of the cod-fishing to the welfare of the Commonwealth."

Tuesday
18
1969—Bernard Moitessier, leading the first race around the world for singlehanded sailors, abandoned the race after crossing his outbound track and continued on to the Pacific islands.

Wednesday
19
1942—Howard Payne Conway, Jr., became the first U.S. Merchant Marine cadet to lose his life in World War II. His ship, the *SS Liberator*, was torpedoed and sunk by a German submarine.

Thursday
20   VERNAL EQUINOX

1943—In one of those strange maritime coincidences, the fishing schooner *Adventure* rammed and sank the fishing schooner *Adventure II* in a fog in Boston Harbor.

Friday
21
1791—John Foster Williams joined the U.S. Revenue-Marine, predecessor of the Coast Guard, and supervised the construction of the first revenue cutter, the *Massachusetts*, whose commander he became.

Saturday
22
1820—U.S. naval hero Stephen Decatur was mortally wounded by James Barron in a duel in Bladensburg, Maryland.

Sunday ○
23   PALM SUNDAY
Knowledge of marlinspike seamanship is what distinguishes the true seaman from the man who merely ventures upon the water at infrequent intervals.
—Boris Lauer-Leonardi

THE REAL LANGUAGE OF THE SEA, ACCORDING TO MARK TWAIN

If the landsman should wish the gang-plank moved a foot farther forward, he would probably say: "James, or William, one of you push that plank forward, please."; but put the mate in his place, and he would roar out: "Here, now start that gang-plank for'ard! Lively, now! *What*'re you about! Snatch it! *snatch* it! There! there! Aft again! aft again! Don't you hear me? Dash it to dash! are you going to *sleep* over it! 'Vast heaving. 'Vast heaving, I tell you! Going to heave it clear astern? WHERE're you going with that barrel! *For'ard* with it 'fore I make you swallow it, you dash-dash-dash-*dashed* split between a tired mud-turtle and a crippled hearse-horse!"

I wished I could talk like that.

SILENT SEASPEAK, ACCORDING TO FILSON YOUNG

Hoists of bunting broke out at yardarms, ascended to mast heads, hovered a minute or two, and came down in rainbow curves where flagship talked to flagship. A shore signal station was speaking in white flashes that dazzled you even in the strong sunshine; and between ship and ship of the same squadron minute conversations, visible only through a strong glass, were being carried ceaselessly on by the busy tossing arms of semaphores and by the small flags that a signalman, perched on the rail of a bridge like a fly, was waving to his opposite number in the next ship.

What were they all saying?

WHAT THEY REALLY SAY, ACCORDING TO JAMES RUNCIMAN

I never yet heard a real conversation among seamen that would bear full reproduction in print. All metaphors, ornaments, literary graces and emphasis are replaced by oaths and improprieties. The man's feeling is measured by the number of naughty words he uses, and the curious thing is that the blasphemer's mind may be essentially healthy and manly. His swearing is innocent, and corresponds to the alliterations and turns of speech with which poets embellish their work.

The respected terminology of marine usage has become a tin-eared cacophony.
—Weston Farmer

THIS IS WHAT COULD HAPPEN IF THEY REALLY SAID IT

Article II. If any shall be heard to swear, curse, or blaspheme the name of God, the Commander is strictly enjoined to punish them for every offense by causing them to wear a wooden collar or some shameful badge, for so long a time as he shall judge proper.   —from the Rules for the Regulation of the Navy of the United Colonies

HEAVEN HELP GUILTY SAILORS DURING RICHARD THE LION-HEARTED'S THIRD CRUSADE IN THE LATE 12TH CENTURY

He who kills a man on shipboard, shall be bound to the dead man, and thrown into the sea; if the man is killed on shore, the slayer shall be bound to the dead body and buried with it. Anyone convicted by lawful witnesses of having drawn his knife to strike another, or who shall have drawn blood of him, he is to lose his hand. If he shall have only struck with the palm of his hand, without drawing blood, he shall be thrice ducked in the sea. Anyone who shall reproach, abuse or curse his companion, shall for every time he is convicted thereof, give him so many ounces of silver. Anyone convicted of theft shall be shorn like a champion, boiling pitch shall be poured on his head and he shall be set ashore at the first land the ship touches.

MARCH

Monday
24

1924—The six-master *Wyoming*, largest wooden schooner ever built, foundered in a storm off Cape Cod. She was built in Bath, Maine, in 1909.

Tuesday
25

The ocean knows no favorites.
        —Samuel Eliot Morison

Wednesday
26

1921—The racing-fishing schooner *Bluenose*, champion of the International Fishermen's Races, was launched at the Smith & Rhuland shipyard, Lunenburg, Nova Scotia.

Thursday
27

The language of the sea is the vernacular of a hard life. —Gershom Bradford

Friday
28 GOOD FRIDAY

1856—The *Sea Witch*, among the first of the tea clippers, struck a reef near Havana, Cuba, and became a total loss.

Saturday
29

1844—Uriah Levy, first Jewish officer in the U.S. Navy, received his captain's commission.

Sunday
30 EASTER

1836—In France, a fiber material was created for the first time from glass. More than 100 years later, it would find its way into boats.

Signalling to moorings

DESIRABLE QUALITIES OF A PERMANENT MOORING

- Heavy enough to hold a vessel of the specified weight and windage in the worst storm possible
- An anchor or weight of an antifouling design
- Placed so it can be picked up no matter the state of weather or the direction of the wind
- Marked so it is visible by day or by night, and in any wave conditions
- Durable enough to go through a season without being hauled for inspection

THE PRINCIPAL FACTORS TO BE CONSIDERED WHEN LAYING A MOORING

1. The nature of the bottom
2. The design, weight, and size of the boat
3. The conditions of the anchorage—exposed or sheltered from the prevailing winds, tidal currents, and wave fetch
4. The amount of swinging room allowed in the anchorage

SHORTER SCOPE MEANS MORE WEIGHT

Many of today's crowded anchorages require a mooring with a short scope. Be sure to increase the weight of the business end of the mooring gear to offset any necessary shortening of the scope.

LENGTH FOR MOORING PENDANT

2½ times the distance from the chock to the waterline

THE ETIQUETTE OF OUTBOARD MOTOR BOATING, ACCORDING TO THE NEW ENGLAND OUTBOARD MOTOR BOATING ASSOCIATION, CIRCA 1930

1. If one who is operating a fast outboard boat sees a rowboat approaching, common courtesy and decency should require that the motor immediately be slowed down so that there will be the least possible ripple and disturbance on the water to the rowboat.
2. If an outboard is being operated in a crowded harbor where yachts are anchored and where people are living aboard, keep away, don't disturb them.
3. If you are at a popular summer resort, do not start your motor until after breakfast at least. There is really no need disturbing everybody's peace from six or seven o'clock in the morning until eleven or twelve at night.
4. There is no necessity for removing mufflers just for the sake of making a little more noise.
5. If you see a man shooting, don't disturb him. If you see a man duck shooting, keep away, give him a chance.

What is important is not so much the size of the gear, but how well designed it is for the purpose. —R.D. "Pete" Culler

MAR/APRIL

Monday
31

1932—The United States signed the International Whaling Convention, endorsed by 21 other nations. The U.S. Coast Guard was assigned the responsibility for enforcing the convention for the United States.

Tuesday
1

1960—A new numbering system for undocumented motorboats on navigable waters was established by the U.S. Coast Guard.

Wednesday
2

1781—The Continental Navy frigate *Alliance* captured two Royal Navy vessels, the *Mars* and the *Minerva*.

Thursday
3

1837—Captain Edwin T. Amesbury, one of the best known of the Down East skippers and master of the down-easter *S.D. Carleton*, was born at North Haven, Maine.

Friday
4

1818—A law went into effect establishing the U.S. flag as having 13 horizontal stripes, with one star for each state of the union.

Saturday
5

1931—W.L. Wyllie, naval and marine artist, died in Portsmouth, England.

Sunday
6

1609—Henry Hudson set sail from Texel, Holland, aboard the *Halve Maen* (*Half Moon*) on a voyage of exploration that would lead to the discovery of the Hudson River.

SPECIFICATIONS FOR JAY GOULD'S MAGNIFICENT STEAM YACHT *ATALANTA*

248 feet 3 inches, length
26 feet 5 inches, beam
16 feet, depth of hold
12 feet, draft
Compound engines, 30-inch low-pressure cylinder, 30-inch stroke, 110 pounds steam, 1,750 indicated horsepower
17 knots, top speed
Hardwood saloons and staterooms

THE LURE OF STEAM YACHTING, ACCORDING TO EDWARD S. JAFFRAY, 1887

The great truth is gradually dawning on the minds of yachtsmen that steam is the perfect motive power. Steam yachtsmen can go where they please, and when they please, and, what is more important, they know when they will get back.

THE FOUR CLASSES OF LATE-19TH-CENTURY STEAM YACHTS AND THEIR ESTIMATED ANNUAL EXPENSES (1887 DOLLARS)

1. Open, undecked launches, $2,500
2. Decked vessels with trunk cabins, $7,500–$10,000
3. Larger yachts with greater depth and a flush deck from stem to stern, $10,000–$12,000
4. Largest yachts with flush decks, year-round accommodations, capable of a circumnavigation, $15,000 and up

I don't know which will eat a man up the quickest, an extravagant wife or a steam yacht, but think of a rich man with both!

—anon.

YACHTING AS COMMUNITY AND PRIVATE SERVICE

None but the comparatively wealthy can own and run a vessel kept purely for pleasure sailing, and it is difficult to see how a man can expend his wealth in sport more profitably to himself, his friends, and the community. In the equipment and victualing of the yacht, all classes of the community receive a share, and the intimate friends of the owner receive that which is most valuable of all, the health-giving exercise and the fresh sea air which is its accompaniment, the owner himself getting in these ample return for all his outlay.   —Captain R.F. Coffin, 1887

DAVID W. BONE, THE ARCHETYPAL MERCHANT SEAMAN, CONSIDERS THE STEAM YACHT

They are too domestic, these laced and powdered darlings. They represent an aristocracy in ships, one that has become indolent and unduly proud, caring for little but the preservation of a fine pose, a graceful and patrician gesture. While one is grateful to the fortunate owner for his fine taste in preserving such a beautiful model, one would like to see him take her to sea more frequently.

Monday
7

1883—Financier Jay Gould's steam yacht *Atalanta*, considered by many to have been the finest yacht built to date in the United States, was launched in Philadelphia.

Tuesday
8

1848—A fleet of prefabricated boats, built for the Lynch Expedition to the Dead Sea and hauled overland by camels, was launched in the Sea of Galilee.

Wednesday
9

1879—Felix Riesenberg, deepwater sailor and author of *Under Sail. Cape Horn*, and other books of the sea, was born in Milwaukee, Wisconsin.

Thursday
10

1872—The first national Arbor Day, dedicated to the planting of trees, was celebrated. Plant more trees; build more wooden boats!

Friday
11

1718—Captain Woodes Rogers, commanding a five-ship squadron, set sail from England on an expedition to the Bahamas to suppress piracy.

Saturday
12

1811—The American merchant vessel *Tonquin* established a trading post at the mouth of the Columbia River, Astoria, Oregon.

Sunday
13

Never has man built any kind of vessel that will ride out any kind of sea. —William Atkin

THE PARTS OF AN OAR
Handle—the hand grip
Loom—the shaft
Throat—the junction of the loom and the blade
Blade—the part that is dipped in the water
Tip—the end of the blade
Leather—the protective covering on the loom

ROWBOATS FOR VARYING CONDITIONS
Total exercise plus speed, flat water—sliding-seat shell
Total exercise plus speed, choppy water—sliding-seat ocean shell
Harbor crawling, utilitarian—flatiron skiff
Harbor crawling, stylish—round-bottomed skiff
Open water, survival—peapod
Fishing, flat water—punt
Fishing, open water—dory
River travel, quiet flat water—long, straight-keeled round-bottomed skiff
River travel, rapids—Mackenzie River boat
All-around elegance—Whitehall

A FEW THOUGHTS ABOUT OARS
The best softwood oars, for lightness and strength, are spruce.
The best hardwood oars, for strength and durability, are ash.
Other oarmaking woods include clear cedar, fir, maple, and basswood.
Ash oars need not be painted or varnished; spruce must be.
Unfinished ash oars can be kept clean and bright by rubbing them down from time to time with sand and canvas.
If the oars are finished, leave the handles bare, as they will be easier to grip.
Good, utilitarian oars should flex during use—not much, but enough to be noticeable. If they are too stiff, thin them down with a spokeshave, paying special attention to the lower end of the loom or shaft near the throat, and the throat itself.
To keep track of a pair of oars matched to a particular boat, paint a design on the blades using the color scheme of the boat. Blue-and-gray boat? Paint blue-and-gray chevrons on the oar blades.

WHEN ROWING IN HEAVY SEA CONDITIONS
Meet the seas end-on, either bow or stern first, to prevent a broach.
Keep way on when meeting a crest, or use the oars to hold the boat. Try to prevent the crest from "grabbing" the boat.
Do not run with the seas unless absolutely necessary. If you must, move weight aft if the bow has a tendency to bury or forward if the transom has a tendency to sink.

GETTING POWER IN YOUR STROKE, FIXED-SEAT ROWING
Center your weight just aft of the center of buoyancy; in other words, the boat should be slightly down by the stern, not by the head.
Back straight; chin up; feet braced against the stretcher.
Do not dig in the blade; keep the upper edge close to the surface.
Pull straight back, with the hands moving in a line parallel to the keel.
Put your back into it—say, half the effort with the back, one-quarter with the arms, and one-quarter with the legs.
At the end of the stroke, pull the elbows tightly into the body.

Monday
14
1912—The White Star liner *Titanic*, on her maiden voyage from Southampton, England, to New York, collided with an iceberg off Newfoundland and sank, with the loss of 1,517 lives.

Tuesday
15
1851—The clipper ship *Flying Cloud*, perhaps the most famous of the type, was launched from the yard of David McKay in East Boston, Massachusetts.

Wednesday
16
1947—The French Liberty ship *Grandcamp* exploded in Texas City, Texas, destroying herself, the cargo ship *Highflyer*, and most of the city.

Thursday
17
1524—Giovanni da Verrazzano, on an exploratory expedition in the caravel *La Dauphine*, landed near a narrows leading to a large bay. Though he named the region Angouleme, it eventually came to be known as New York.

Friday
18
1775—Paul Revere crossed by rowboat from Boston to Charlestown, Massachusetts, on the first leg of his famous ride to Lexington.

Saturday
19
There is no such thing as the superior, all-purpose rowboat, just as there is no such animal as the superior, all-purpose dog. —John Gardner

Sunday
20
1951—Adolf Hitler's 476-foot yacht *Grille*, a spoil of war, was towed from Brooklyn, New York, to a wrecker's yard in Bordentown, New Jersey.

THE FOULEST PORT

Experience has shown that the amount of fouling is greater in the tropics than in higher latitudes, and in the summer and early fall than at any other time of year. The port that has the most unenviable reputation in this respect is Surabaya, and it is stated that vessels lying there for a week at any period of the year will become foul, though covered with the best anti-fouling paint ever made. Other ports in Java are of like evil repute, and ships in the ports of the Malabar Coast, and on the Madras Coast, and in Ceylon, foul very readily during eight months of the year.
—from *The Navigator or Mariners' Guide*, 1905

THREE WAYS TO WORK ON A BOAT'S BOTTOM WITHOUT HAULING HER

1. Tie her up next to a pier or wharf and let the tide run out from under her.
2. Run her in to a sandy beach and secure her with anchors forward and aft so she is parallel with the shore. As the tide falls, careen her toward the beach with lines out to an anchor, or a convenient tree, or a deadman. To work on the other side of the bottom, turn the boat at the next high tide.
3. Run her in to a sandy beach, bow-on; as the tide falls, steady her upright with "legs" on each side or with shoring of an appropriate sort.

THE BASIC TYPES OF MODERN COPPER ANTIFOULING PAINT

Rosin—soft, low abrasion resistance, moderate antifouling protection; good for slow-speed craft in northern climates; least expensive type

Resin, or resin-rosin combination—semi-hard, moderate abrasion resistance, moderate antifouling protection; good for average boats with average use; moderately expensive

Vinyl—hard, tough, smooth finish, with moderate antifouling protection; ideal for racing craft; expensive

Epoxy—hard, tough, high abrasion resistance, moderate antifouling protection; good for boats launched from trailers or on and off a beach; expensive

Copolymer—moderately hard, good abrasion resistance, good antifouling protection; good protection for craft that see hard use in warmer climates; expensive

Water-based—moderately hard, low abrasion resistance, moderate antifouling protection; less disagreeable to apply because of lack of chemical solvents; moderately expensive

OLD-STYLE RECIPE FOR HOMEMADE BOTTOM PAINT

1 pound red lead
4 ounces copper bronze powder
4 ounces arsenic
4 ounces chrome yellow
4 ounces Paris blue
1 pint driers
1 pint boiled linseed oil
1 pint copal varnish

If too thick, add more varnish.

IN A PINCH . . .

Any paint can be made somewhat antifouling by adding a healthy slug of the nastiest ground red pepper you can find.

Monday
21

There is nothing sordid, cramped, or unhealthy for body or mind in what a man may learn from sailing boats.
—H. Warington Smyth

Tuesday
22

PASSOVER BEGINS

1858—The clipper ship *James Baines* caught fire and burned while unloading cargo in Liverpool, England. Her hulk was later converted to a landing stage.

Wednesday
23

1680—A band of 68 buccaneers in canoes attacked three Spanish warships with a total of 228 men in Panama City, Panama, and captured them all.

Thursday
24

1961—The 64-gun ship *Vasa*, sunk in 1628, was raised from the bottom of Stockholm Harbor, Sweden. After years of restoration and conservation, she is now a historical exhibit.

Friday
25

1719—*The Life and Strange and Surprising Adventures of Robinson Crusoe*, by Daniel Defoe, was published in London, England.

Saturday
26

1956—The converted T-2 tanker *Ideal X*, the first containership— loaded with modern, standardized containers—departed Port Newark, New Jersey, for Houston, Texas.

Sunday
27

1969—David Pyle and one crew member set sail from England in the 18-foot Drascombe lugger *Hermes*. They arrived in Australia 341 days later at the end of the longest open-boat cruise to date.

THE FIRST FOUR STEAMSHIPS OF THE CUNARD LINE, ORIGINALLY KNOWN AS THE BRITISH AND NORTH AMERICAN ROYAL MAIL STEAM PACKET COMPANY

Britannia, paddle-wheeler, 207 feet, 1,156 tons, 423 hp

Columbia, paddle-wheeler, 207 feet, 1,138 tons, 425 hp

Acadia, paddle-wheeler, 206 feet, 1,136 tons, 425 hp

Caledonia, paddle-wheeler, 206 feet, 1,138 tons, 425 hp

All four vessels averaged about 8.5 knots.

THE GROWTH IN SIZE OF THE LARGEST TRANSATLANTIC LINERS IN THE YEARS PRECEDING WORLD WAR I

1902, *Celtic*, 20,904 tons

1906, *Kaiserin Auguste Victoria*, 24,581 tons

1908, *Mauretania*, 31,938 tons

1911, *Olympic*, 43,324 tons

1912, *Imperator*, 52,226 tons

1914, *Leviathan*, 59,957 tons

MOST OF THE GREAT STEAMER LINES FOLLOWED A PATTERN WHEN NAMING THEIR SHIPS

Cunard Line—almost all ended in "ia," as the *Servia, Gallia, Umbria, Cephalonia, Etruria*, etc.

White Star Line—all ended in "ic," as the *Celtic, Germanic, Britannic, Adriatic, Republic, Titanic*, etc.

Royal Mail Steam Packet Company—most were named after rivers, as *Thames, Trent, Dee, Medway, Moselle, Tagus*, etc.

Inman Line—almost all were named after cities, as the *City of Richmond, City of Chester, City of Berlin, City of Chicago*, etc.

Anchor Line—almost all were named after geographic regions, as the *Asia, Armenia, Assyria, Australia, Britannia, Caledonia*, etc.

Allan Line—almost all ended in "ian," as the *Caspian, Carthaginian, Nova Scotian, Parisian, Sarmatian*, etc.

Canadian Pacific Line—the largest had "Empress" in their names, as *Empress of Britain, Empress of Australia, Empress of Canada, Empress of Russia*, etc.

Prince Line—named after princes, as *Moorish Prince, Arabian Prince, Siamese Prince*, etc.

Bibby Line—named after English counties, as *Derbyshire, Staffordshire, Shropshire*, etc.

THE MAJOR MODERN COMMERCIAL SHIP-CLASSIFICATION SOCIETIES

- American Bureau of Shipping, United States
- Det Norske Veritas, Norway
- Lloyd's Register of Shipping, United Kingdom
- Germanischer Lloyd, Germany
- Nippon Kaiji Kyokai, Japan
- Registro Italiano Navale, Italy

THE ULTIMATE SHIPS

They are the perfection in ship-craft of the builder, these great liners designed exclusively for mail and passenger services. In them there is expressed every sound calculation, every brilliant pound of reasoning, every provision that a hard practical experience has handed down through centuries of trial.

—David W. Bone

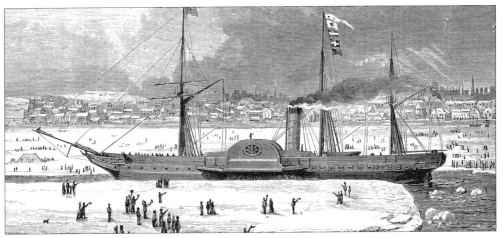

The first Cunard steamer Brittania at Halifax.

To a landsman a ship's name means not a thing. Listen, then—Euphrosyne, Lady Isobel, Eurydice, Cambrian Chief, Melanope. —Bill Adams

APRIL/MAY

Monday
28

1865—Sir Samuel Cunard, founder of the Cunard Line, died in England.

Tuesday
29

Praise a small vessel, but put your cargo in a large one. —Hesiod

Wednesday
30

1988—*The Pride of Baltimore II*, a replica of a Baltimore clipper built to replace an earlier reproduction lost at sea in 1986, was launched in Baltimore, Maryland.

Thursday
1

1863—The schooner-yacht *America*, taken into the U.S. Navy, was ordered to Newport, Rhode Island, for service as a training vessel for midshipmen at the U.S. Naval Academy.

Friday
2

1835—The Hudson's Bay Company's *Beaver*, the first steamship on the west coast of North America, was launched in Blackwall, River Thames, London, England.

Saturday
3

1983—The original old block shop of A. Dauphinee & Son, Lunenburg, Nova Scotia, makers of blocks and fittings for the fishing fleet, was closed.

Sunday
4

Just as there are landsmen on shore who never set foot in a boat if they can help it, so there are watermen who never work ashore unless forced to do so. —Varley Lang

COAL BUNKERS ABOARD STEAM VESSELS

Normal space allowance for stowing coal: 45 cubic feet per ton

North Country (of England) or "small" coal: 43 cubic feet per ton

Large Welsh coal: 45 cubic feet per ton

"Duff," or fine coal screenings: 41 cubic feet per ton

KEEPING THE COAL FIRES BURNING

Long ocean passages in 19th-century steamships required immense stockpiles of fuel at coaling stations around the world, and a great number of colliers were required to keep the stocks topped up. In the mid-19th century, for example, the Peninsula and Oriental Steam Navigation Company (the P & O), which ran from Britain to the Far East, maintained coaling stations at the following locations:

Southampton, 2,000 tons
Malta, 5,000 tons
Alexandria, 6,000 tons
Aden, 20,000 tons
Bombay, 8,000 tons
Point de Galle, 12,000 tons
Madras, 5,000 tons
Calcutta, 4,000 tons
Singapore, 8,000 tons
Hong Kong, 10,000 tons
Yokohama, 2,000 tons
King George's Sound, 4,000 tons
Sydney, 1,500 tons

IF IT LOOKS LIKE ONE, IT IS ONE

I was on deck on the starboard side aft about 2 p.m. talking with Mr. Bloomfield, of New York, and Mr. Deerberg, of London, when I saw what looked like a whale or a porpoise rising about three-quarters of a mile to starboard. We all knew what it was, but no one named it.

Immediately a white line, a train of bubbles, started away from the black object. No one spoke until it was about sixty yards from the submarine, then Deerberg said, "It looks like a torpedo." Bloomfield said, "My God! it *is* a torpedo!"

—statement of a passenger aboard the RMS *Lusitania*

Oh, where are you going to, all you big
*   steamers,*
With England's own coal, up and down the salt
*   seas?*
We are going to fetch you your bread and your
*   butter,*
Your beef, pork, and mutton, eggs, apples, and
*   cheese.*
For the bread that you eat and the biscuits you
*   nibble,*
The sweets that you suck and the joints that
*   you carve,*
They are brought to you daily by all us big
*   steamers,*
And if any one hinders our coming you starve.
                        —Rudyard Kipling

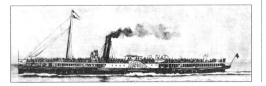

[The sea] detests cowardice and is a friend to those who know and respect her; but on the other hand she is likely to chasten flippancy or over-familiarity with pitiless severity. —William Washburn Nutting

MAY

Monday
5

1886—The extreme six-beam cutter *Oona* (34 feet long, 5½ feet wide) was wrecked on the Irish coast during her maiden voyage, with all hands drowned. The disaster contributed to the demise of the Tonnage Yacht Rating Rule, favoring plank-on-edge hulls.

Tuesday
6

1936—The U.S. Congress authorized the construction, in Carderock, Maryland, of the David W. Taylor Model Basin for tank-testing hull shapes.

Wednesday
7

1915—The Cunard Liner RMS *Lusitania*, underway from New York for Liverpool, was torpedoed and sunk off southern Ireland by the German submarine *U-20*, with the loss of more than 1,100 lives.

Thursday
8

1870—At the zenith of the age of sail, Captain Boultbee Whall counted 300 sailing vessels in sight of the Lizard, at the entrance to the English Channel.

Friday
9

1910—The Gloucester fishing schooner *Elsie*, which would be defeated by the Lunenburger *Bluenose* in the second International Fishermen's Race (1921), was launched in Essex, Massachusetts.

Saturday
10

1797—The *United States*, first frigate of the U.S. Navy, was launched in Philadelphia, Pennsylvania.

Sunday
11

1937—*Ranger*, greatest of the J-class yachts, designed by Starling Burgess and Olin Stephens, was launched in Bath, Maine.

A TRUE AND VERITABLE SEA SERPENT OFF NOVA SCOTIA

We beheld at the distance of from 150 to 200 yards on our starboard bow, the head and neck of some denizen of the deep.... The creature rapidly passed, leaving a regular wake, from the commencement of which, to the forepart, which was out of the water, we judged its length to be about 80 feet; and this is within rather than beyond the mark. We were, of course, all taken aback at the sight, and with staring eyes and in speechless wonder stood gazing at it for full half a minute; there could be no mistake, no delusion, and we were all perfectly satisfied that we had been favored with a view of the "true and veritable sea serpent," which had been generally considered to have existed only in the brain of some Yankee skipper, and treated as a tale not much entitled to belief.

> —from the sworn testimony of five British army officers, 1833

THE CRY OF THE WHALEMAN

"Whale! Whale!"
"Thar blows!"
"She blows!"
"There she blows!"
"Blows! Blows! There blows!"
"Blo-o-o-ows!"

THE TOIL OF THE BORED WHALER, ACCORDING TO HERMAN MELVILLE

Throughout the Pacific, and also in Nantucket, New Bedford, and Sag Harbor, you will come across lively sketches of whales and whaling scenes graven by fishermen themselves on sperm whale teeth....in general they toil with jack-knives alone and with that almost omnipotent tool of the sailor, they will turn out anything you please in the way of a mariner's fancy.

NATURE'S PROOF OF A NORTHWEST PASSAGE, ACCORDING TO HERMAN MELVILLE

It is a thing well known to both American and English whaleships...that some whales have been captured far north in the Pacific, in whose bodies have been found the barbs of harpoons darted in the Greenland seas.

INSCRIPTION ON A 19TH-CENTURY SCRIMSHAW CORSET BUSK OR STAY

Accept, dear Girl this busk from me;
  Carved by my humble hand.
I took it from a Sparm Whale's Jaw,
  One thousand miles from land!
In many a gale,
Has been the Whale,
      In which this bone did rest,
        His time is past,
        His bone at last
          Must now support
            thy brest.

He looked about to see that there were no listeners, and said, in a very earnest voice, that the king of the fish was the sea-serpent. —John Masefield

MAY

Monday
12
1797—Mutiny broke out aboard HMS *Sandwich* at The Nore, mouth of the River Thames, England. Eventually the rebellion spread to the rest of the fleet in the anchorage, only to collapse a few weeks later.

Tuesday
13
1870—The hulk of HMS *Beagle*, which had carried Charles Darwin on his voyage of scientific discovery, most recently a watch vessel on the coast of Essex, England, was sold for scrap.

Wednesday
14
1986—The *Pride of Baltimore*, a reproduction of a Baltimore clipper, was knocked down by a freak squall and sank with the loss of four lives in the Atlantic Ocean north of Puerto Rico.

Thursday
15
1833—Five officers of the British army, on a fishing expedition out of Halifax, Nova Scotia, spotted a giant sea serpent.

Friday
16
1866—The keel of John MacGregor's second Rob Roy canoe was laid. MacGregor, the father of double-paddle canoeing, used the boat for a grand tour of northern Europe.

Saturday
17
1870—In a clean sweep of a three-race match, the American schooner *Sappho* defeated the British schooner *Cambria* off the Isle of Wight, thus avenging a humiliating loss two years earlier.

Sunday
18
1845—HMS *Erebes* and *Terror*, commanded by Sir John Franklin, set sail from England in search of the Northwest Passage. They never returned, nor did their crews.

Vasco da Gama

SAILORS' NAMES FOR THE THREE GREAT SOUTHERN CAPES, AS CONRAD CALLED THEM, "THAT LOOK UPON THE GALES"

The Cape—the Cape of Good Hope, known by Vasco da Gama as The Cape of Storms

The Horn—seldom referred to by deepwater sailors by its formal name, Cape Horn

Cape Leeuwin—always referred to by its full name, "as if," wrote Joseph Conrad, "to console its second-rate dignity"

THE MIGHTY HOOD GOES DOWN

Suddenly, the *Hood* split in two, and thousands of tons of steel were hurled into the air. More than a thousand men died. Although the range was still about 18,000 meters, the fireball that developed where the *Hood* still was seemed near enough to touch. It was so close that I shut my eyes but curiosity made me open them again a second or two later. It was like being in a hurricane. Every nerve in my body felt the pressure of the explosions. If I have one wish, it is that my children may be spared such an experience.

—Korvettenkapitan Wolf Neuendorff, navigator of the *Bismarck*

THE BOOKS OF MAURICE GRIFFITHS

Nonfiction

Yachting on a Small Income (1925)
The Magic of the Swatchways (1932)
Ten Small Yachts and Others (1933)
Little Ships and Shoal Waters (1937)
Cruising Yarns from the 'Y.M.' (1938)
Post-War Yachting (1945)
Dream Ships (1949)
Everyman's Yachting (1952)
Sailing on a Small Income (1953)
The Arrow Book of Sailing (1966)
Swatchways and Little Ships (1971)
The First of the Tide (1979)
Round the Cabin Table (1985)
Sixty Years a Yacht Designer (1988)

Fiction

Dempster and Son
No Southern Gentleman
Sands of Sylt

THE PROGRESS OF PORTUGUESE MARITIME DISCOVERY IN THE 15TH CENTURY

1418, Madeira
1446, Cape Verde Islands
1449, Azores
1463, West Africa to the Equator
1487, Cape of Good Hope (Bartholomew Diaz)
1498, India (Vasco da Gama)

LEFTIES WILL LOVE THIS

In the Portuguese navy, the port side of a ship is designated the "honor side" in memory of Vasco da Gama, who doubled the Cape of Good Hope by keeping Africa at all times on the port side.

Cape Horn

It takes several years for anyone to learn to handle a yacht reasonably well, and a lifetime to admit how much more there is to learn. —Maurice Griffiths

MAY

Monday
19
1896—Congress passed an Act to allow the Secretary of the Treasury, administrator of the Revenue-Cutter Service, to regulate yachting regattas on navigable waters. The act was intended primarily to keep clear the America's Cup course.

Tuesday
20
1498—Vasco da Gama, Portuguese navigator, landed at Calicut on the Malabar Coast; he was the first to round the Cape of Good Hope and the first European to cross the Indian Ocean.

Wednesday
21
1876—George Webber Mixter, author of the *Primer of Navigation*—known to its adherents simply as "Mixter's"—was born in Rock Island, Illinois.

Thursday
22
1902—Maurice Griffiths, yacht designer, editor of *Yachting Monthly*, and author of *The Magic of the Swatchways*, among other books, was born in South London, England.

Friday
23
1701—Captain William Kidd, convicted of piracy, was hanged at Execution Dock, Wapping, London, England.

Saturday
24
1941—A shell from the German battleship *Bismarck* penetrated an ammunition room of the British battle cruiser *Hood*, exploded, and sank the ship within minutes. Only three survived.

Sunday
25
1918—Three small coasting schooners were damaged by a marauding German submarine off Cape Charles, Virginia.

THE MEETING OF THE SHIPS
by Thomas Moore

When o'er the silent seas alone,
For days and nights we've cheerless gone,
Oh, they who've felt it know how sweet,
Some sunny morn a sail to meet!

Sparkling at once is every eye,
"Ship ahoy! ship ahoy!" our joyful cry;
While answering back the sounds we hear,
"Ship ahoy! ship ahoy! what cheer? What
*   cheer?"*

Then sails are backed; we nearer come:
Kind words are said of friends and home;
And soon, too soon, we part with pain,
To sail o'er silent seas again.

A MOST MOVING MOMENT, ACCORDING TO FRANCIS CHICHESTER

At 1520 the huge aircraft carrier HMS *Eagle* passed close by, with her crew lining the deck and giving *Gipsy Moth* three cheers. I dipped my ensign in salute. This was a great honour, which I found most moving. It must surely be unique in the history of the British Navy for a warship with a complement as big as the population of a small town to salute so ceremoniously a ship with a crew of one!

THE ACHIEVEMENTS* OF SIR FRANCIS CHICHESTER IN HIS SOLO VOYAGE AROUND THE WORLD

- Fastest voyage around the world by a yacht
- Longest nonstop passage, 15,500 miles, by a small sailing vessel
- Most miles run in a week by a singlehander
- Greatest number of miles run per day by a yacht on a long passage—for 107 days, 131¾ miles per day; for 119 days, 130¼ miles per day
- Third true circumnavigation, including a passage around the Horn, by a small vessel

* As of May 1967; some of these records have since been surpassed.

A GHOST OF THE PAST, AS SEEN BY H.M. TOMLINSON

What was wrong?

"Nothing, sir; the chief officer wants you on the bridge."

I went up hurriedly, in pyjamas and oilskins. Day had not come, but it was not night; night was lifted slightly in the east on a wedge of rose, though the wind was still bleak out of the darkness. We were somewhere near the Berlengas [Portugal]. What was this? My friend the chief officer pointed astern without a word. We were passing a ghost ship, under all canvas. The barque was so close that I could see the length of her deck. She was silent, and more pale than the twilight. She was tall, and tinctured faintly with rose. Had we steamed back into another age? Was the past so near? I could see two men on her poop, but they were not looking at us. Only my friend, and the bridge of our liner, were material. My friend spoke. "I thought you would like to see her; it may be the last time. Isn't she a beauty?"

For 99.999 (recurring) percent of mankind, dreams remain locked up in the secret compartments of the soul. Not for Chichester.   —J.R.L. Anderson

MAY/JUNE

Monday
26   MEMORIAL DAY

1940—A fleet of "Little Ships" began the evacuation of the British Expeditionary Force from the beaches of Dunkirk on the Strait of Dover.

Tuesday
27

1911—Victor Emerson's motorboat *Furlong* became the first watercraft to make good a speed greater than 40 mph. She achieved 42.5 mph on the Potomac River.

Wednesday
28

1967—Francis Chichester returned to Plymouth, England, completing the first one-stop single-handed circumnavigation of the globe, a voyage of 29,670 miles in 226 sailing days. Total elapsed time was nine months and a day.

Thursday
29

1898—As the ice went out on Lake Bennett, Yukon Territory, in the spring of the great Klondike Gold Rush, 7,124 homemade boats pushed off down the Yukon River en route to Dawson City.

Friday
30

1921—The Gloucester fishing schooner *Esperanto*, winner of the first International Fishermen's Race a year earlier, struck the submerged wreck of a steamer off Sable Island, Nova Scotia, and sank.

Saturday
31

1853—The first U.S. expedition to the Arctic got underway from New York.

Sunday
1

1815—The Yacht Club, later the Royal Yacht Club, the first of its type in England, was established during a meeting at the Thatched House Tavern, St. James's Street, London.

FEAR CAN BE A GOOD THING

A man who is not afraid of the sea will soon be drownded...for he will be going out on a day he shouldn't. But we do be afraid of the sea, and we do only be drownded now and again.

—from *The Playboy of the Western World*, by J.M. Synge

SAFETY AT SEA IS NOT A MATTER OF SIZE ALONE, ACCORDING TO WINTHROP P. MOORE

It is a matter of proper rig and design of the vessel, experience in the crew, and a skipper who knows what has to be done and who has the confidence to put that knowledge into practice.

PRECAUTION IS THE WATCHWORD, SAYS FLEET ADMIRAL CHESTER NIMITZ, USN

The time for taking all measures for a ship's safety is while still able to do so. Nothing is more dangerous than for a seaman to be grudging in taking precautions lest they turn out to have been unnecessary. Safety at sea for a thousand years has depended on exactly the opposite philosophy.

NEVER UNDERESTIMATE MURPHY'S LAW, ESPECIALLY AT SEA, SAYS H.W. TILMAN

In our enthusiasm we began shortening the passage [in our minds] by days or even weeks, but I deprecated too much optimism by enumerating all the accidents which might happen to us, including even the breaking of the boom. Sure enough the next day it did break.

THE HAND ON THE TILLER IS THE KEY, ACCORDING TO CAPTAIN A. J. KENEALY

There are many types of boat and each has some peculiar attribute to recommend it. No two craft, for instance, could be more widely different in every way than a Gloucester fishing dory and a Cape Cod catboat, yet each when properly handled has safely ridden out an Atlantic gale. Of course if their movements had been directed by farm hands both would have foundered.

A LIFE LOST, ANOTHER GAINED

In attempting this voyage I risked losing a life that had at last become fulfilling; but in carrying it out I experienced a second life, a life so separate and complete it appeared to have little relation to the old one that went before.
                                          —Naomi James

FACT, NOT THEORY, ACCORDING TO CARL D. LANE

No boat need strand on a strange coast if the skipper is a navigator and seaman in fact, not theory.

No boat need suffer a "licking" at sea if the skipper is a seaman and sailor in fact, not theory.

No boat need suffer any form of shipwreck if her skipper has fitted her out and equipped her for the purposes of her use, wisely and generously.

It must not be forgotten even in the finest weather that there is no such thing as "playing at sailors" when at sea. —C.E. Seth-Smith

JUNE

Monday
2

1958—The *Raymond*, the last working wooden narrowboat built in Britain, was launched at Samuel Barlow's boatyard, Braunston, Northamptonshire, England.

Tuesday
3

1839—Herman Melville, author of *Moby-Dick* and other novels, shipped out for the first time. He took a berth as a deckhand aboard the sailing vessel *St. Lawrence*, carrying cotton from New York to Liverpool.

Wednesday
4

1966—John Ridgway and Chay Blyth set out from Orleans, Massachusetts, to row across the Atlantic to Britain in the 20-foot Yorkshire dory *English Rose III*.

Thursday
5

1794—The U.S. Congress set the territorial limits of the United States at three miles. The United States was the first country to make such an official declaration.

Friday
6

1813—Captain James ("Don't Give Up the Ship") Lawrence, USN, mortally wounded in the battle between the USS *Chesapeake* and HMS *Shannon*, was buried in Halifax, Nova Scotia. His body was later removed to the cemetery at Trinity Church, New York City.

Saturday
7

1978—New Zealander Naomi James, in the 53-foot cutter *Express Crusader*, returned to England via Cape Town and the Falklands, thus becoming the first woman to sail around the world alone.

Sunday
8

1813—Admiral David Dixon Porter, U.S. naval hero of the American Civil War, was born in Chester, Pennsylvania.

HEY, CAPTAIN, TAKE A LOOK AT THIS!

This morning one of our companie looking over boord saw a mermaid, and calling up some of the companie to see her, one more came up and by that time shee was come close to the ships side, looking earnestly on the men. A little after a sea came and overturned her. From the navill upward her backe and breasts were like a womans, as they say that saw her, but her body as big as one of us. Her skin very white, and long haire hanging downe behinde of colour blacke. In her going downe they saw her tayle, which was like the tayle of a porposse, and speckled like a macrell. Their names that saw her were Thomas Hilles and Robert Rayner.

— Henry Hudson

The unobserving man is always stupid; it is the want of observation that dampens and deadens his faculties. — Conrad Miller

TWO TYPES OF BINOCULARS

Galilean—two joined-together telescopes, one for each eye, using normal lenses

Prismatic—two joined-together telescopes, one for each eye, using lenses and a series of prisms

FEATURES TO CONSIDER WHEN CHOOSING BINOCULARS OR A SPYGLASS

- Power of magnification
- Definition and brightness of view
- Field of vision

The more the power of magnification, the less the field of vision.

BINOCULAR RATINGS

Binoculars are rated by magnification, or "power," and by the diameter in millimeters of the lens, known as the objective lens, farthest from the eyepiece. A binocular rated as 7 x 35 has a magnification of seven times and an objective lens of 35 millimeters diameter.

FAVORED BINOCULARS

7 x 50—generally best for all-purpose marine use; excellent at night and in poor visibility; overly bright in clear visibility

7 x 35—excellent in clear visibility

6 x 30—same as 7 x 35, but with a wider field of view

TO CLEAN TELESCOPE OR BINOCULAR LENSES

Gently blow off loose dirt and grit.

Breathe on the lens and polish with a clean tissue.

Or polish with a clean proprietary lens paper.

MY BOAT

Children's song lyrics by Edna Cobb Dutcher

I watched the big boat sail out to the sea,
One fine day in September.
She'll voyage they say,
Two months and a day,
And come sailing home in November.

My father commands, the sailors obey;
No captain ever was grander;
And when I am grown,
A vessel I'll own,
And stand on the bridge as commander.

There is nothing sordid, cramped, or unhealthy for body or mind in what a man may learn from sailing boats. —H. Warington Smyth

JUNE

Monday
9

1949—The 73-foot yacht *Bolero*, designed by Sparkman & Stephens, three-time winner of the Bermuda Race, was launched at the Nevins shipyard, City Island, New York.

Tuesday
10

1853—The famed clipper ship *Young America* set sail from New York for San Francisco on her maiden voyage.

Wednesday
11

1954—Charles Francis Adams III, yachtsman, racing skipper, secretary of the navy under Herbert Hoover, died.

Thursday
12

1725—John Peck, designer of the famed merchant vessel *Empress of China* and the first American naval architect to specialize in design rather than design and construction, was born in Boston, Massachusetts.

Friday
13

1813—The *Chesapeake*, first steamboat on Chesapeake Bay, got underway on her first voyage, from Baltimore to Annapolis, Maryland.

Saturday
14

1777—John Paul Jones was appointed commander of the Continental Navy cruiser *Ranger*.

Sunday
15

1608—Henry Hudson, on a voyage seeking a northeast passage to the Indies, reported that two of his crew sighted a mermaid.

Nat Herreshoff, designer of the catamaran Amaryllis.

THE MULTIHULL IS NOT AS NEW TO YACHTING AS SOME BELIEVE

The first catamaran to enter a yacht race was the *Amaryllis*, designed and built by Nathanael G. Herreshoff. She easily beat all comers, including some of the fastest boats in the country, in the second race of the 1876 Centennial Series, held to celebrate the 100th anniversary of United States independence. After seeing for himself the success of the *Amaryllis* and after following the exploits of other catamarans of the late 19th century, yachting journalist Captain R.F. Coffin opined as follows:

"As an open yacht, the catamarans are superior to all others in every way. They are faster, safer, handier. They will not only sail fast; but they will lie still. There is one gentleman who has owned more of these craft than any one else, who is so expert in handling them, that he can do with them what cannot, without great risk, be done with any other description of open yachts; that is, weave in and out among the steamers and sailing craft of the most crowded part of the river front, and make a landing without the least damage. He has run side by side with the swiftest of the harbor steamers and beaten them, and has frequently gone the whole length of Long Island Sound with only a small boy as crew."

SOME OF THE MANY ACHIEVEMENTS OF ISAMBARD KINGDOM BRUNEL (1806-1859)

- Design and construction of Britain's Great Western Railway
- Design of the paddle steamer *Great Western*, the first steamship built specifically for transatlantic crossings
- Design of the steamer *Great Britain*, the first large oceangoing ship with a screw propeller
- Design of the steamer *Great Eastern*, the largest ship of her time, the first ship with a double bottom, powered with a unique paddle-wheel/screw combination
- Design and engineering of many of the great British commercial docks and piers of the time, particularly in Bristol, Plymouth, and Milford Haven
- Design of a floating gun carriage for use in the Crimean War

SPECIFICATIONS OF THE *GREAT EASTERN*

Length between perpendiculars, 680 feet
Length of upper deck, 692 feet
Beam, 83 feet
Breadth across paddle boxes, 118 feet
Depth, deck to keel, 58 feet
Number of decks, 4
Tonnage, 28,093 tons
Number of anchors, 10
Number of boats, 20
Number of watertight compartments, 12
First-class passengers, 800
Second-class passengers, 2,000
Third-class passengers, 1,200
Number of saloons, 10
Length of principal saloon, 100 feet

THE *GREAT EASTERN* AS COMPARED TO NOAH'S ARK, CALCULATIONS FOR THE LATTER ACCORDING TO SIR ISAAC NEWTON

Length between perpendiculars—Noah's Ark, 515.62 feet; *Great Eastern*, 680 feet

Breadth—Noah's Ark, 89.94 feet; *Great Eastern*, 83 feet

Depth—Noah's Ark, 51.56 feet; *Great Eastern*, 58 feet

Tonnage—Noah's Ark, 18,232 tons; *Great Eastern*, 28,093 tons

For the actual sailing, I enjoyed these craft
[catamarans] more than any I ever owned.
—Nathanael G. Herreshoff

JUNE

Monday
16

*One of the excellentest artes that ever
hath bin devised is the arte of navigation.* —Martin Frobisher

Tuesday
17

1860—The huge iron passenger steamer
Great Eastern, the wonder of her age,
designed by Isambard Kingdom Brunel,
sailed on her maiden voyage from
Southampton, England, for New York.

Wednesday
18

1541—Hernando DeSoto and a
party of Spanish explorers, having
built four piraguas, crossed the
Mississippi River for the first time.

Thursday
19

1876—The first U.S. Lifesaving Medal
was awarded to Lucian M. Clemons,
keeper of the U.S. Life-Saving Service
station, Marblehead, Ohio, for valor in
saving the crew of the schooner *Consuelo*.

Friday ◯
20

1872—The flying start was used for
the first time in a yacht race sponsored
by the New York Yacht Club.

Saturday
21   SUMMER SOLSTICE

1767—HMS *Dolphin*, commanded by
Captain Samuel Wallis, discovered
the island of Tahiti.

Sunday
22

1877—The revolutionary catamaran
Amaryllis, designed and built by
Nathanael G. Herreshoff, drove her
bows under and pitchpoled while sailing at great speed in a match race.

SPEED-TIME-DISTANCE FORMULAS
Distance = Speed x Time
Speed = Distance/Time
Time = Distance/Speed

CONJECTURE VS. SCIENTIFIC MEASUREMENT, ACCORDING TO CLAUD WORTH

A few days before starting on a cruise we dined with Green's uncle, a retired Naval officer. We told him about a very smart run which Foam had made from Weymouth to the Needles, and Green estimated the speed at eight and a half knots. A day or two afterwards a box arrived at Green's lodgings containing a log-ship [chip log] with line, reel, and sand-glass. Foam was faster than most yachts of her size. All day, with a strong southwest wind she travelled at very nearly her maximum speed. We hove the log several times. On one occasion only her speed just reached six knots. A log-ship is a most instructive instrument.

TO THE *PURITAN*
by J.D. Logan

A gallant Ship of Speed that swept the sea,
Fearless, confident, and proud and free!
O hapless Ship of Beauty that had no flaw,
Too soon a prey to Ocean's avid maw.

We sorrow that an envious, ruthless Fate
Marked thee to be the Esperanto's mate;
And meet the self-same, swift unworthy
*   doom*
Where Sable's treacherous waters loudly
*   boom!*

Had Ocean spared thee and thy gallant crew,
We should have seen thee come into thy
*   due—*
Speed champion of the waters, or win fame,
And add new glory to thy Gloucester's name!

But Hearts Courageous still in Gloucester
*   dwell;*
Their souls are brave, their wills undaunt-
*   able;*
Another Puritan will rise at length,
And ride the seas with greater speed and
*   strength.*

THE LOG LINE

The traditional log line consists of a line with a chip or float at the end, wound onto a freely turning reel. A white rag is tied in the line at a distance of 12 fathoms from the chip. Following the white rag, knots are tied in the line at 47¼-foot intervals. This log line is used with a sandglass timed at 28 seconds, or, more often in the modern era, a stopwatch. The float is thrown overboard and when the white rag reaches the taffrail, the sandglass is inverted or the stopwatch started. The number of knots that passes the taffrail by the time the sand in the glass runs out, or the stopwatch indicates 28 seconds, equals the vessel's speed in nautical miles per hour, or, as the old-time navigators called it, knots per hour.

The faster the mile, the more it costs.
—R.D. "Pete" Culler

JUNE

Monday
23

1922—The three-month-old Gloucester fishing schooner *Puritan*, thought to have been the fastest of her type ever built but too short-lived to prove it, was wrecked on a reef off Sable Island, Nova Scotia.

Tuesday
24

1954—The speed launch *Whippet II* threw a piston rod while going more than 75 mph on Salt Pond, Chatham, Massachusetts; hot metal blew a hole through the hull below the waterline, sinking the boat in less than 30 seconds.

Wednesday
25

1916—Artist Thomas Eakins, painter of *The Pair-Oared Shell* and other works with a rowing theme, died in Philadelphia, Pennsylvania.

Thursday
26

1870—The first seaside boardwalk in the United States was opened in Atlantic City, New Jersey.

Friday
27

1865—John MacGregor's first double-paddle canoe, the original Rob Roy, was launched. A synthesis of the Native American canoe and the Inuit kayak, it was the first of its type.

Saturday
28

1860—I.K. Brunel's passenger ship *Great Eastern*, later a cable-layer, arrived in New York at the end of her maiden voyage from Southampton, England.

Sunday
29

1920—Work commenced on a great dam across the mouth of the Zuider Zee, Holland, to keep the lowlands from flooding and to create the Ijsselmeer.

THE SECRET TO KEEPING DECK SEAMS TIGHT

Slosh down with seawater as often as possible—at least every morning, midday, and evening.

OLD-STYLE RECIPE FOR ELASTIC MARINE GLUE FOR PAYING SEAMS

1. Gently heat 1 part india rubber with 12 parts coal tar in a kettle.
2. Add 20 parts shellac.
3. Apply while hot and runny.

A HOMEMADE LUBRICANT TO KEEP THE THREADS OF FITTINGS FROM SEIZING UP

Mix together equal amounts of tallow, graphite grease, spar varnish, and white or red lead. Smear on the threads.

FROM A SAN FRANCISCO NEWSPAPER, JULY 1852

One of the most beautiful harbor sights that has occurred here for some time came off yesterday. The magnificent clipper *Hoogly*, which had been lying at the end of Broadway Wharf, loosed her sails about noon, cast off her lines, swept away majestically from the end of the wharf and put directly to sea.... She carries a crew of 25 men; they were all on board at the appointed hour; the jib, foretopsail and maintopmast staysail were loosed; the bow line cast off. The ship leaned over and shot swiftly away without accident.

OLD-STYLE METHOD OF CANVASING THE WOODEN DECK OF A YACHT

Plane the deck planking smooth.

Cut the canvas to shape.

Make bedding compound by boiling together 10 pounds rosin, 2 gallons linseed oil, and 10 pounds tallow.

Spread compound on deck, then lay canvas in it.

Stretch canvas taut and fasten around the edges with copper tacks.

Go over the canvas with a hot laundry iron; the heat will drive the compound into the canvas and the decking.

Screw down wooden moldings bedded in compound along the edges and along any seams.

Apply two coats of paint.

TO MAKE TALLOW

1. Place twice as much animal fat in a large pot as the amount of tallow desired.
2. Add enough fresh water to fill the pot nearly to the top.
3. Bring to a boil, then cover and simmer for at least 12 hours.

The purified fat—tallow—will rise to the top. Skim it off and throw away the remainder.

TITLES CONSIDERED BY KENNETH GRAHAME BEFORE SETTLING ON *THE WIND IN THE WILLOWS*

The Wind in the Reeds
Down Stream
With the Stream
The Lapping of the Stream
The Babble of the Stream
By Pleasant Streams
The Whispering Reeds
The Children of Pan
Under the Alders
Reeds and Rushes
Reeds of the River
By Waters Fair
In the Sedges
River Folk

I have read [The Wind in the Willows] and re-read it, and have come to accept the characters as old friends.
                                        —Theodore Roosevelt

JUNE/JULY

Monday
30

1967—The jet-powered *Hustler*, driven by Lee Taylor, Jr., on Lake Guntersville, Alabama, became the first powerboat to make a speed greater than 285 mph.

Tuesday
1

1852—In an extraordinary feat of seamanship, the 200-foot clipper ship *Hoogly* departed Broadway Wharf, San Francisco, under sail alone, without assistance. Seven weeks later, she stranded in Shanghai.

Wednesday
2

1812—The first steam-powered ferryboat service was inaugurated in New York Harbor by Robert Fulton. The new ferry *Jersey* ran from New York City to Paulus Hook, New Jersey.

Thursday
3

Ladies will be admitted to the main Club House after 3 p.m. on Thursdays during July and August when there is music.
          —Rules of the Eastern Yacht Club, Marblehead, Massachusetts, 1914

Friday
4 INDEPENDENCE DAY

1912—Joseph Anis, a dory fisherman working out of Boston, Massachusetts, caught a codfish whose stomach contained a glass eye.

Saturday
5

1932—Kenneth Grahame, author of *The Wind in the Willows* and the immortal line "There is nothing—absolutely nothing—half so much worth doing as simply messing about in boats," died in Pangbourne, England.

Sunday
6

1787—The first-known iron vessel, built by John Wilkinson in Willey, Shropshire, England, was launched.

Morgan at Porto Bello

MORGAN
by Edmund Clarence Stedman

Oh, what a set of Vagabundos,
  Sons of Neptune, sons of Mars,
Raked from todos otros mundos,
  Lascars, Gascons, Portsmouth tars,
Prison mate and dock-yard fellow,
  Blades to Meg and Molly dear,
Off to capture Porto Bello,
  Sailed with Morgan the Buccaneer!

Out they voyaged from Port Royal
  (Fathoms deep its ruins be,
Pier and convent, fortress loyal,
  Sunk beneath the gaping sea);
On the Spaniard's beach they landed,
  Dead to pity, void of fear, —
Round their blood-red flag embanded,
  Led by Morgan the Buccaneer.

Dawn till dusk they stormed the castle,
  Beat the gates and gratings down;
Then, with ruthless rout and wassail,
  Night and day they sacked the town,
Staved the bins its cellars boasted,
  Port and Lisbon, tier on tier,
Quaffed to heart's content, and toasted
  Harry Morgan the Buccaneer.

Stripped the church and monastery,
  Racked the prior for his gold,
With the traders' wives made merry,
  Lipped the young and mocked the old,
Diced for hapless senoritas
  (Sire and brother bound anear),
Donnas, Inas, Manuelitas,
  Cursing Morgan the Buccaneer.

Lust and rapine, flame and slaughter,
  Forayed with Welshman grim:
"Take my pesos, spare my daughter!"
  "Ha! ha!" roared that devil's limb,

"These shall jingle in our pouches,
  She with us shall find good cheer.
Lash the graybeard till he crouches!"
  Shouted Morgan the Buccaneer.

Out again through reef and breaker,
  While the Spaniard moaned his fate,
Back they voyaged to Jamaica,
  Flush with doubloons, coins of eight,
Crosses wrung from Popish varlets,
  Jewels torn from arm and ear, —
Jesu! how the crimps and harlots
  Welcomed Morgan the Buccaneer!

THE NAVAL AND MARITIME BOOKS OF SAMUEL ELIOT MORISON

The Maritime History of Massachusetts, 1921
Portuguese Voyages to America in the Fifteenth Century, 1940
Admiral of the Ocean Sea: A Life of Christopher Columbus, 1942
History of U.S. Naval Operations in World War II, 15 volumes, 1947-62
By Land and by Sea, 1953
Christopher Columbus, Mariner, 1955
John Paul Jones: A Sailor's Biography, 1959
The Two-Ocean War, 1963
The Caribbean as Columbus Saw It (with Mauricio Obregon), 1964
Spring Tides, 1965
Life of Commodore Matthew C. Perry, 1794-1858, 1967
The European Discovery of America, The Northern Voyages A.D. 500-1600, 1971
Samuel de Champlain, Father of New France, 1972
The European Discovery of America, The Southern Voyages A.D. 1492-1616, 1974

I'm a jolly pirate, out for gold,
I will rummage through your hold.
                                    —anon.

JULY

Monday
7
1876—The schooner-yacht *America*
went aground, suffering much damage,
on Brigantine Shoals off the coast of
New Jersey. Later, she was pulled off
by salvagers and repaired.

Tuesday
8
1886—Mary E. Coons became the
first woman to be issued a license
for operating a steam vessel, the
launch *Elizabeth*, in the East River
and New York Bay, New York.

Wednesday
9
1887—Maritime historian Samuel
Eliot Morison, author of *The
Maritime History of Massachusetts*
and other works, was born in
Boston, Massachusetts.

Thursday
10
1899—The schooner-yacht *Cambria*, America's
Cup challenger and winner of the famous 1870
race across the Atlantic with the *Dauntless*, was
broken up for scrap. She had spent her last days
trading on the coast of Guinea, West Africa.

Friday
11
1668—A party of 500 buccaneers, led
by the pirate Henry Morgan, ransacked
the city of Portobello, Cuba.

Saturday
12
*A day in the life of a sailor offers
more adventure than the average
man experiences in his entire lifetime.*   —Charles G. Davis

Sunday
13
1814—The *New Orleans*, first
steamboat on the Mississippi River,
became impaled on a stump near
Baton Rouge and sank when she
was pulled off.

THE SHOCK OF THE SHORE

Then, as if the furies of the sea and wind were freed at last to end their coquetry, they lifted us—high, high above the ledge—and dropped us there. And the impact of that shock was only less than those that followed for that half an hour until *Direction* sank.

—Rockwell Kent

WHEN WAVES BECOME DANGEROUS

A strong wind blows against, or at a sharp angle to, a pre-existing swell.

A strong wind blows against a strong tide.

A shoal rises suddenly out of deep water.

The wind becomes so strong as to blow off the tops of the waves.

THE THREE PRINCIPAL DANGERS OF RUNNING BEFORE A HEAVY SEA

1. The vessel can broach—that is, a wave can catch the stern and slew the vessel broadside to the seas.
2. The vessel can be pooped—that is, a high, green sea can be taken over the stern.
3. The vessel can be pitchpoled—that is, a wave can lift the stern while driving the vessel forward with such speed that her bow is driven down, causing a somersault.

If any of these dangers seem likely, it is time to heave-to.

THE VERY FIRST ACTIONS TO BE TAKEN IN AN EMERGENCY

Fire—man the fire extinguishers; maneuver the vessel so the fire is on the leeward side.

Collision—man the pumps.

Abandon ship—distribute the lifesaving devices and make sure everyone puts them on.

Man overboard—throw a lifesaving device; point at the person in the water and keep pointing at him for the benefit of the navigator.

TO REMOVE SURVIVORS FROM A SINKING VESSEL

Approach the sinking vessel from leeward, come alongside, fend off, and prepare to push away in an emergency.

Be aware of wreckage in the water, especially anything that can foul the propeller, and be wary of loose rigging and falling objects from the sinking vessel.

If it is unsafe for the survivors to drop directly into the rescue boat, have them jump into the water first and then pull them aboard. Be sure they don life preservers before jumping and, if possible, have a lifeline attached, which will make pulling them alongside that much easier.

Yacht sailors, as a rule, are sober, honest,
obliging, good-tempered, original.
     —Sir Edward Sullivan

JULY

Monday
14
1986—David Scott Cowper embarked in the 42-foot motor lifeboat *Mabel E. Holland* from Newcastle, England, on a circumnavigation of the globe during which he would become the first to make a solo transit of the Northwest Passage.

Tuesday
15
1929—The cutter *Direction*, with artist Rockwell Kent and two others aboard, was wrecked on the western coast of Greenland.

Wednesday
16
1845—The first regatta of the New York Yacht Club was held, during which a time-allowance system was used for the first time in the United States. Winner on elapsed time was William Edgar's *Cygnet*.

Thursday
17
1972—The Wood Neck Marine Antiques Exchange in Sippewissett, Massachusetts, settled out of court with the Acme Foundry and Machine Shop, Belleville, North Dakota, over an alleged patent infringement involving a case-hardened gronicle.

Friday
18
1606—The Portuguese navigator Luis Vaez de Torres discovered a passage, now known as the Torres Strait, between the south coast of New Guinea and the northern tip of Australia.

Saturday ○
19
1845—The first open yacht race to be sailed east of Cape Cod was held in Massachusetts off Nahant. The schooner *Cygnet* was first over the line; the winner on time allowance was the schooner *Raven*.

Sunday
20
1876—The 141-foot extreme centerboard schooner *Mohawk* capsized in a squall in New York Harbor. Owner William Garner, his wife, and three others drowned.

TOWING THE TENDER

Fix the towing line to a stem ring close to the waterline of the boat being towed. This provides lift to the bow and keeps the forefoot from digging in.

If the tender has a tiller rigged, lash it at an angle that will keep the boat running straight.

Experiment with the length of the towing line. The goal is to have the bow of the towed boat rising on the back of a following wave.

A boat that doesn't tow well can sometimes be modified by adding a deeper or longer skeg, or by adjusting the trim with movable ballast, or by dragging a length of line astern aligned with the centerline of the boat.

America crossing the Atlantic

FOUR WAYS TO CARRY A TENDER ON A CRUISING BOAT, IN DESCENDING ORDER OF SAFETY

1. Lashed upside down on deck
2. Carried right side up on deck
3. Carried right side up in davits
4. Towed astern

If carried on deck, be sure it is stowed in a place that will not interfere with the work of the deck crew, especially in heavy weather. The lashings should take into account the worst weather possible.

If carried right side up, either in chocks on deck or in davits, cover with a waterproof canvas secured for the worst weather possible. A boat filled with water on deck will have an adverse effect on the center of gravity.

If carried in davits, secure the boat so it will not swing.

If towed astern, use a stout towing line secured to a structural bitt at the stern and running over the stern through a chock or fairlead. Protect the line from chafe.

OLD-FASHIONED METHOD OF CURING A LEAKING CARVEL - OR LAPSTRAKE- PLANKED DINGHY

When the boat has been out of the water long enough to dry, scrape and sand away all loose and flaking paint. It is not necessary to get all the way down to the bare wood, but it helps.

With the boat out under a hot sun, liberally brush on a coat of raw, not boiled, linseed oil. Carefully work the oil into the seams between the planks and along the rabbet line. Do not wipe off the excess oil.

Allow the wood to take up the oil over several days, then repeat the process.

Wait several more days, then wipe off any excess oil with an absorbent cloth and rub down the surface with a cloth soaked in turpentine.

After a week or so, when the surface has dried, paint or varnish the boat.

The oil will have swelled the wood and tightened the seams.

A DEAD BOAT IS A DEAD BOAT, SAYS GEORGE PUTZ

You can get a season or two out of her by running a cotton yarn into the seams with a putty knife; not like you're caulking, you understand, just run it in there and make good contact. Then get a tube of Instant Patch or some other asphalt-based gunk and fair it into the seams with your finger, running the finger along the seam fast enough to create some pressure. Then tap and back each fastening a couple of times and paint with porch-and-deck enamel. When the paint is dry, run the garden hose into the boat and keep water in her for a day or two and put her overboard when she quits watering the lawn. Don't kid yourself; the boat's still dead.

Monday
21

1588—The first shots of the running battle
between the English fleet and the Spanish
Armada were fired off the Eddystone Light,
near Plymouth, England.

Tuesday
22

1926—The *Charles W. Morgan*, last of the
New England whalers, was established as a
memorial to the whaling industry in New
Bedford, Massachusetts. She is now exhib-
ited at Mystic Seaport, Connecticut.

Wednesday
23

1887—Joshua Slocum, captain of
the bark *Aquidneck*, then moored
in Antonina, Brazil, killed one man
and wounded another. Pleading
self-defense, he was acquitted.

Thursday
24

1978—The 92-foot ketch *Whitehawk*,
designed by Bruce King, scaled up from L.
Francis Herreshoff's 72-foot *Ticonderoga*,
at the time the largest cold-molded yacht,
was launched in Rockland, Maine.

Friday
25

1866—David Glasgow Farragut
became the first U.S. naval officer
to hold the rank of admiral.

Saturday
26

1859—The first intercollegiate rowing
regatta in the United States was held
on Lake Quinsigamond, Worcester,
Massachusetts. Harvard defeated Yale
and Brown over a three-mile course.

Sunday
27

1918—The first concrete barge, the
98-foot *Socony 200*, was launched
in Flushing Bay, New York.

BURSTS OF SPEED

Given the proper conditions, the clippers in their heyday recorded astonishing bursts of speed:

22 knots—*Sovereign of the Seas*, October 23, 1854

21 knots—*James Baines*, June 18, 1856

20 knots—*Champion of the Seas*, December 12, 1854

19 knots—*Great Republic*, December 12, 1856

18.5 knots—*Marco Polo*, January 7, 1854; *Flying Cloud*, July 31, 1851

18 knots—*Donald McKay*, February 27, 1855; *Sweepstakes*, February 11, 1854

THE PROPER CONDITIONS FOR SPEED, ACCORDING TO CARL CUTLER

The first requirement—and one rarely realized—was that the ship should be lightly loaded to her best sailing marks. For one clipper to put to sea in fair racing trim, a hundred were heavily overloaded. Another requisite was that the ship's bottom should be clean and smooth—a condition which presupposed recent docking. A strong but extremely steady following wind, which raised a smoothly rolling, but powerfully driving sea, was equally essential. This latter condition was not only rare, but of brief duration as a rule. Usually, strong winds were puffy, which necessitated reducing sail voluntarily or, in the alternative, "by Act of God." They also stirred up a dangerous, lumpy sea. A shipmaster might sail for a lifetime without once meeting the ideal combination of conditions for attaining the full potential speed of his ship.

FAST AS A WHIPPET AND COMFORTABLE TO BOOT, FROM A CONTEMPORARY DESCRIPTION OF THE CLIPPER SHIP *FLYING CLOUD*

We can only say that more comfortable luxury, more tasteful and costly furniture, more ample ventilation and comfort of every kind, we never knew even in an earth-built packet ship or steamer.

The *Flying Cloud* is just the kind of vehicle, or whatever else it may be called, that a sensible man would choose for a ninety days voyage.

THE COLOR SCHEME OF THE CLIPPER SHIP *FLYING CLOUD*

Black—bowsprit, channels, hull above the copper sheathing

White—deckhouses, railcap and monkey rail, inside the bulwarks, small boats

Light blue—waterways, tops of deckhouses

Scraped and/or varnished—masts, jib-boom beyond bowsprit end, yards, decks

ECONOMICS KILLED THE CLIPPER SHIP

Generally speaking, before the 1880s fast ships carried small cargoes. In the 1880s new, slower ships were built to carry large cargoes, and the true clipper became obsolete.

*If there is one place in the world of Romance,
it is under tropical skies in a sailing ship.*
—Arthur Mason

JULY/AUG

Monday
28
1778—Rear Admiral Charles Stewart,
U.S. naval hero of the War of 1812 and
commander of the frigate *Constitution*
during her victory over HMS *Levant*,
was born in Philadelphia, Pennsylvania.

Tuesday
29
1969—The Great Lakes schooner *Alvin Clark*,
sunk in Lake Michigan's Green Bay in 1864,
was raised intact. Unsuccessful as a land-
based tourist attraction, she was bulldozed
in May 1994 to make way for a parking lot.

Wednesday
30
1844—The New York Yacht Club,
first in the United States, was established aboard the yacht *Gimcrack*
off the Battery, New York Harbor.

Thursday
31
1878—The Andrews brothers, William
and Asa, landed at Mullen Cove, Cornwall,
England, in their 19-foot dory *Nautilus*
after crossing the Atlantic from South
Boston, Massachusetts.

Friday
1
1851—The clipper *Flying Cloud*, on her
maiden voyage to California, logged a
new record, soon to be broken by several clippers, of 374 nautical miles for
the day, an average of nearly 16 knots.

Saturday
2
1866—Charles Francis Adams III,
yachtsman, racing skipper, secretary
of the navy under Herbert Hoover,
was born in Quincy, Massachusetts.

Sunday
3
1816—Ferdinand Rudolph Hassler
was appointed the first superinten-
dent of the U.S. Coast Survey.

THE LOSS OF THE *KON-TIKI*, ACCORDING TO THOR HEYERDAHL

The *Kon-Tiki* was wholly changed, as by the stroke of a magic wand. The vessel we knew from weeks and months at sea was no more; in a few seconds our pleasant world had become a shattered wreck....

I was completely overwhelmed. I sank down on my knees and thrust my fingers deep down into the dry warm sand.

The voyage was over. We were alive.

THE J CLASS

J-class yachts were light-weather craft, designed only for racing. There was a joke among yachtsmen during the heyday of the Js that the skipper would set a lighted candle on the boom at night. If the flame remained in the morning, the weather was too calm for a race; if it was out, there was too much wind for a race.

THE THREE MAJOR ELEMENTS CONSIDERED BY ALMOST ALL RACING-YACHT RATING RULES

1. Length of hull
2. Sail area
3. Displacement

By jiggering around these components, some rating rules encourage speed at the expense of seaworthiness, or extreme design over common sense, or the ability to race and cruise successfully, or some other combination of qualities—some desirable, some not.

WEIRD BUT PRODUCTIVE, ACCORDING TO DOUGLAS PHILLIPS-BIRT

The progress of sailing yacht architecture has been for part of its time the wayward and often eccentric changes in design produced by unforeseen mathematical quirks in the [racing] measurement rule in force.... [Yet] most of the notable developments in yacht architecture were the product of faulty rules that for a moment in their history allowed profitable experiments in design to be made.

American yachting needs less common sense, less restrictions, less slide rules, and more sailing.   —William Washburn Nutting

THE SUCCESSFUL AMERICA'S CUP DEFENDERS FROM THE BOARD OF OLIN J. STEPHENS II OF THE DESIGN FIRM SPARKMAN & STEPHENS

Ranger, J class, co-designed with Starling Burgess

Columbia, 12-Meter
Constellation, 12-Meter
Intrepid, 12-Meter (defended twice)
Courageous, 12-Meter (defended twice)
Freedom, 12-Meter

When the winds of July and August blow,
The masts of most of the J-class go. —anon.

AUGUST

Monday
4

1880—The American Canoe Association held its first regatta on Lake George, New York. W.P. Stephens won the first race, for paddles in sailing canoes; T.H. Wallace won the second, for paddles in paddling canoes.

Tuesday
5

1937—In the last race to involve huge J-class yachts for the America's Cup competition, *Ranger* of the New York Yacht Club defeated *Endeavour II* of the Royal Yacht Squadron, sweeping the series 4-0.

Wednesday
6

Boatbuilders are often very conservative, because they have to deal with the safety of the men who go in the boats.
            —T.C. Lethbridge

Thursday
7

1947—Thor Heyerdahl's 45-foot balsa-log raft *Kon-Tiki* was wrecked on Raroia Reef, Tuamotu Islands, after sailing from Callao, Peru, to prove that the Polynesians could have emigrated from South America.

Friday
8

1870—*Magic* was successful in the first defense of the America's Cup. She defeated *Cambria* of the Royal Thames Yacht Club.

Saturday
9

1848—Captain Frederick Marryat, author of *Mr. Midshipman Easy, Peter Simple,* and *The Pirate,* among other novels of the sea, died in Norfolk, England.

Sunday
10

1675—The naval observatory in Greenwich, England, was founded. Eventually its site would mark the position of 0 degrees longitude.

THE FIRST VOYAGE OF THE *CLERMONT,* ACCORDING TO HER INVENTOR, ROBERT FULTON, IN A LETTER TO A FRIEND

Robert Fulton

My steamboat voyage to Albany and back has turned out rather more favorable than I had calculated. The distance from New York to Albany is one hundred and fifty miles; I ran it up in thirty-two hours, and down in thirty. I had a light breeze against me the whole way, both going and coming, and the voyage has been performed wholly by the power of the steam engine. I overtook many sloops and schooners beating to windward, and parted with them as if they had been at anchor. The power of propelling boats by steam is now fully proved. The morning I left New York there were not, perhaps, thirty persons in the city who believed that the boat would even move one mile an hour, or be of the least utility; and while we were putting off from the wharf, which was crowded with spectators, I heard a number of sarcastic remarks. This is the way in which ignorant men compliment what they call philosophers and projectors.

STEAM SIMPLY WILL NOT WORK TO PROPEL BOATS, ACCORDING TO THE EMINENT ENGINEER BENJAMIN H. LATROBE IN A PAPER DELIVERED TO THE AMERICAN PHILOSOPHICAL SOCIETY IN 1803

There are, indeed, general objections to the use of the steam-engine for impelling boats, from which no particular mode of application can be free. These are:

First. The weight of the engine and of the fuel.

Second. The large space it occupies.

Third. The tendency of its action to rack the vessel and render it leaky.

Fourth. The expense of maintenance.

Fifth. The irregularity of its motion, and the motion of the water in the boiler and cistern, and of the fuel-vessel in rough water.

Sixth. The difficulty arising from the liability of the paddles or oars to break, if light, and from the weight if made strong.

FROM H. FREELAND'S EYEWITNESS REPORT ON THE FIRST VOYAGE OF FULTON'S *CLERMONT*

A knot of villagers was gathered on a high bluff just opposite Poughkeepsie, on the west bank of the Hudson, attracted by the appearance of a strange dark-looking craft, which was slowly making its way up the river. Some imagined it to be a sea-monster, whilst others did not hesitate to express their belief that it was a sign of the approaching judgment . . . .

On her return trip, the curiosity she excited was scarcely less intense—the whole country talked of nothing but the sea-monster, belching forth fire and smoke. The fishermen became terrified, and rowed homewards, and they saw nothing but destruction, devastating their fishing grounds; whilst the wreaths of black vapor, and rushing noise of the paddle-wheels, foaming with the stirred up waters, produced great excitement amongst the boatmen.

Departure of the Clermont on her first voyage.

Monday
11

He who lets the sea lull him into a false
sense of security is in very grave danger.
                    —Hammond Innes

Tuesday
12
1947—Bowdoin B. Crowninshield, naval architect, designer of the America's Cup contender
Independence, the fishing schooner *Rob Roy*,
and the seven-masted schooner *Thomas W.*
Lawson, died in Marblehead, Massachusetts.

Wednesday
13
1912—The U.S. Congress passed an
Act to Regulate Radio Communications,
which required all operators and stations, including those aboard ships at
sea, to be licensed.

Thursday
14
1834—The brig *Pilgrim*, with Richard
Henry Dana, Jr., aboard, set sail on a
voyage from Boston, Massachusetts,
around Cape Horn, to California.

Friday
15
1925—The first Fastnet Race got underway from the Isle of Wight, England, to
the Fastnet Rock off Ireland, and back.
The winner was the converted Le Havre
pilot boat *Jolie Brise*.

Saturday
16

What makes a boy dream about the sea
is as mysterious as what makes him
dream at all.   —Jan de Hartog

Sunday
17
1807—Robert Fulton's steamboat *Clermont* got up steam for
her historic voyage from New
York City to Albany and back.

An old whaler

THE FATE OF A ROGUE WHALE

Five months after the *Ann Alexander* was rushed and sunk by a vengeful leviathan, the whaler *Rebecca Sims* of New Bedford captured a large whale. Buried in the body were two of the *Ann Alexander*'s irons, and embedded in the head were several pieces of the vessel's timbers.

THE 14 BRITISH YACHTS DEFEATED BY THE SCHOONER *AMERICA* IN THE RACE AROUND THE ISLE OF WIGHT FOR THE HUNDRED-GUINEA CUP

Brilliant, schooner, 392 tons
Constance, schooner, 218 tons
Wyvern, schooner, 205 tons
Alarm, cutter, 193 tons
Beatrix, schooner, 161 tons
Gypsey Queen, schooner, 160 tons
Arrow, cutter, 84 tons
Mona, cutter, 82 tons
Bacchante, cutter, 80 tons
Ione, schooner, 75 tons
Freak, cutter, 60 tons
Eclipse, cutter, 50 tons
Volante, cutter, 48 tons
Aurora, cutter, 47 tons

A BRITISH NAVAL ARCHITECT ON THE VICTORY OF THE SCHOONER-YACHT *AMERICA*

America reaped a crop of glory; England reaped a crop of wisdom. It was worth the loss of a race to gain so much.

SIC TRANSIT GLORIA MUNDI

In the early 1980s, a schism developed within the sanctioning body of the Eastern States Quick-Draw Yacht-Design Competition over the use of pocket calculators. Most of the leading quick-draw designers—the Establishment—were adamantly opposed to the use of these devices. The newer generation, the Young Bloods, had grown up with electronic calculators and counted their use indispensable; though excellent draftsmen, they were unable to perform the necessary trigonometric calculations in their heads. The so-called Compromise of 1984 allowed the use of calculators in the time trials, but not in the finals. The net result was that the Establishment, led by C. Montmorency Jute, T.P. Wendell Butte, and Esteban T.L. McQuark—all excellent old-style mathematicians but totally outclassed when it came to modern yacht design—retained the upper hand in the 1984 finals by virtue of their ability to do calculations without modern electronic devices. The Young Bloods, excellent designers, humiliated by their inability to prove it, walked out during the presentation of the Perpetual Trophy, which in 1984 was jointly won by Messrs. Butte and McQuark. With the compromise effectively compromised, interest in the competition withered and died.

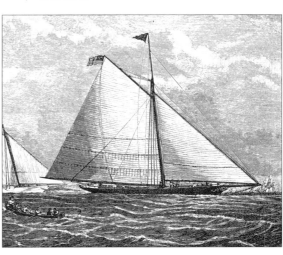

Let me roll around the globe, let me rock upon the sea; let me race and pant out my life with an eternal breeze astern and an endless sea before!
—from *Redburn*, by Herman Melville

Monday ○
18
1959—The scow schooner *Alma* was floated off a mudflat by Roger Olmsted, Karl Kortum, and Harry Dring. She would be restored, eventually sail again, and become part of the fleet of historic ships in San Francisco.

Tuesday
19
1808—Fredrik Henrik af Chapman, shipbuilder and author of *Architectura Navalis Mercatoria*, died in Karlskrona, Sweden.

Wednesday
20
1851—The whaleship *Ann Alexander* of New Bedford was sunk by a whale in the mid-Pacific. The whale smashed two boats and chased a third to the ship, which it rushed, breaking a hole in the bottom.

Thursday
21
1918—The Gloucester fishing schooners *A.P. Andrew* and *Francis J. O'Hara, Jr.*, and the Canadian schooner *Una A. Saunders*, were boarded by a crew from the German submarine *U-156* off Nova Scotia and dynamited.

Friday
22
1851—The schooner-yacht *America* won the Hundred-Guinea Cup, later known as the America's Cup, by beating 14 yachts of the Royal Yacht Squadron in a race off Cowes, Isle of Wight, England.

Saturday
23
1985—The Eastern States Quick-Draw Yacht-Design Competition, established in 1900, was officially discontinued after a schism developed in the governing body over the use of pocket calculators in the finals.

Sunday
24
1927—A great gale struck the fishing banks off Nova Scotia, sinking among other vessels the racing-fishing schooner *Columbia*, which disappeared with 22 men, the most lives lost in a single vessel out of Gloucester.

The wreck of the Royal George

THE LOSS OF THE *ROYAL GEORGE*
by William Cowper

Toll for the brave —
The brave! that are no more:
   All sunk beneath the wave,
Fast by their native shore.
   Eight hundred of the brave,
Whose courage well was tried,
   Had made the vessel heel
And laid her on her side;
   A land-breeze shook the shrouds,
And she was overset;
   Down went the Royal George,
With all her crew complete.

Toll for the brave —
Brave Kempenfelt is gone,
   His last sea-fight is fought,
His work of glory done.
   It was not in the battle,
No tempest gave the shock,
   She sprang no fatal leak,
She ran upon no rock;
   His sword was in the sheath,
His fingers held the pen,
   When Kempenfelt went down
With twice four hundred men.

   Weigh the vessel up,
Once dreaded by our foes,
   And mingle with your cup
The tears that England owes;
   Her timbers yet are sound,
And she may float again,
   Full charged with England's thunder,
And plough the distant main;
   But Kempenfelt is gone,
His victories are o'er;
   And he and his Eight hundred
Must plough the wave no more.

WHY GO?

The Horn was the big attraction in a voyage round the world. For years it had been in the back of my mind. It not only scared me, frightened me, but I think it would be fair to say that it terrified me. The accounts of the storms there are, quite simply, terrifying . . . . I hate being frightened, but, even more, I detest being prevented by fright.
                                    —Sir Francis Chichester

BAD LUCK GEORGE, BAD LUCK CHARLOTTE

Two ships of the Royal Navy were named after King George III and his queen, Charlotte. Both were unlucky. On August 29, 1782, the *Royal George* capsized and sank at Spithead. On March 17, 1800, the *Queen Charlotte* caught fire off the Mediterranean island of Cabrera, burned to the waterline, and capsized with the loss of 673 lives.

OMENS OF BAD LUCK

   Black cats, which were thought to carry gales in their tails
   Sailors from Scarborough, England, whose wives allegedly kept black cats at home to protect their husbands' lives at sea
   The sighting of a whale, which meant gales of wind would follow
   Dreaming of white horses at night, which would produce a blow the next day
   The shadow of one person crossing that of another on deck
   Rats leaving a leaking ship
   Taking over as master of a ship after her skipper died on the previous voyage
   Sleeping on deck in the light of the moon, which would make you moonstruck, or crazy

Sunday sail, never fail
Friday sail, ill luck and gale.
— anon.

AUGUST

Monday
25

1807—Commodore Edward Preble, USN, naval hero and commander of the USS *Constitution*, died.

Tuesday
26

1845—The *Great Britain*, largest steamer then afloat and the first ship with a screw propeller to cross the Atlantic, departed Liverpool, England, for New York, on her maiden voyage.

Wednesday
27

1966—Francis Chichester departed from Plymouth Hoe, England, on his epic one-stop singlehanded circumnavigation; rounding Cape Horn was his greatest single goal.

Thursday
28

1911—The first gyrocompass on an American naval vessel was installed aboard the USS *Delaware*.

Friday
29

1782—The British warship *Royal George* sank suddenly at her moorings in Portsmouth Harbor, England, while being careened for repairs below her waterline. Most of her crew was lost.

Saturday
30

The occasion that moved mee to take such a voyage in hand, was onely a curiositie of minde, a desire of novelties, and a longing to learne out the bounds of the Ocean.
— Lucian of Samothrace

Sunday
31

1861—The daily issue of rum for enlisted men in the U.S. Navy was abolished.

SHIPBUILDING WAS ONE OF THE MAJOR REASONS WHY THE UNITED STATES EMERGED VICTORIOUS IN WORLD WAR II

Between 1940 and 1945, the United States engaged in the largest shipbuilding program ever undertaken. Besides the vessels already in the fleet, the U.S. Navy acquired 1,556 new large combatant and auxiliary vessels, among them:

10 battleships
31 aircraft carriers
49 heavy and light cruisers
969 destroyers, destroyer escorts, and frigates

In addition, there were built:

4,099 landing ships and craft
3,444 small vessels and auxiliaries

Other armed services added to the total, among them:

6,698 wooden and steel tugs, small craft, and barges for the Army
324 cutters, tenders, and icebreakers for the Coast Guard

Meanwhile, the Maritime Commission oversaw the construction of 5,171 new cargo vessels, among them:

2,710 Liberty ships
531 Victory ships
525 T-2 tankers
210 C1-M-AV1 diesel cargo ships

Me—and Halsey and Nimitz
Are anchored in Tokyo Bay
The place is just dripping
American shipping
They stretch for a hell of a way
We hear that the fighting is finished
And that is the way it should be
Remember Pearl Harbor—they started it then
We're warning them never to start it again
For we have a country with millions of men
Like Nimitz and Halsey—and me.
　　　　　　　　—Captain W.G. Beecher, Jr., USN

CONSIDERATIONS WHEN ANCHORING IN A STRANGE HARBOR, ACCORDING TO JOHN "ROB ROY" MACGREGOR

You sail into a port where in less than a minute you must apprehend by one panoramic glance the positions of twenty vessels, the run of the tide, and set of the wind, and depth of the water; and this not only as these are then existing, but, in imagination, how they will be six hours hence, when the wind has veered, the tide has changed, and the vessels have swung round, or will need room to move away, or new ones will have arrived.

TO DETERMINE IF THE ANCHOR IS DRAGGING

Pick a fixed object on the shore and check every minute or so to see if the bearing changes (take into consideration, however, the swinging of the vessel).

Put your hand on the rode ahead of the bow chock; if the rode is vibrating, the anchor is dragging.

Lower a lead line to the bottom and, with the line quite slack, secure it to the rail; if the line comes taut, the anchor is dragging (take into consideration, however, the effect of a rising tide).

SOLUTIONS FOR A DRAGGING ANCHOR

Let out more scope.
Deploy a second anchor.
Reset.

SEPTEMBER

Monday
1 LABOR DAY

1945 [U.S. time]—Japan formally accepted the terms of surrender aboard the U.S. battleship *Missouri*, anchored in Tokyo Bay, thus ending World War II.

Tuesday
2

1890—The giant, five-masted steel bark *France*, 3,784 gross tons, 361 feet long, 49,000 square feet of sail, was launched.

Wednesday
3

1913—The *George W. Wells*, the first six-masted schooner, went ashore on Cape Hatteras, North Carolina, during a hurricane and was wrecked.

Thursday
4

If the gods are good and permit you to build your Perfect Ship, I warn you not to let yourself be too much disappointed when you first see her afloat.
—Weston Martyr

Friday
5

1776—The first official regulations for uniforms of the Continental Navy were issued by the Marine Committee of the Continental Congress.

Saturday
6

1841—The whaler *Charles W. Morgan*, now an exhibit at the Mystic Seaport Museum, departed from New Bedford, Massachusetts, on her first whaling voyage.

Sunday
7

1846—A severe coastal storm struck North Carolina's Outer Banks with such fury that the tidal surge created a new, navigable channel through the barrier beach of Cape Hatteras.

CONTRARY TO POPULAR PERCEPTION, THE SUN DOES NOT RISE IN THE EAST

. . . except during those rare times when its declination is 0 degrees—i.e., when it will become straight overhead at midday.

At all other times, it will rise north of east when the sun is north of the equator and south of east when the sun is south of the equator.

THE METHODS OF NAVIGATION

Piloting—fixing position within sight of land or aids to navigation

Celestial navigation—fixing position by reference to the sun, the moon, various planets, and various stars

Dead (deduced) reckoning—determining approximate position by plotting courses and distances from the last positive position determined by either piloting or celestial navigation

Electronic navigation—fixing position by such electronic devices as radar, radiobeacons, Loran, GPS, and others

IN THE ATLANTIC OCEAN, A GOOD NAVIGATOR HAS THIS QUALITY, SAYS ALF LOOMIS

The ability to distinguish sunrise from sunset, then to steer toward the sunset until a large continent looms in sight.

LORAN-C, GPS, AND OTHER ELECTRONIC SYSTEMS ARE FINE, BUT . . .

- The receivers are delicate instruments that depend on electricity to keep them functional.
- Use them with the understanding that sooner or later they will go on the fritz
- Therefore, ALWAYS KEEP A DEAD-RECKONING PLOT.

REMEMBER THIS WHEN READING THE COMPASS

The compass card does not move. Rather, the boat, as represented by the lubber's line on the bowl of the compass, moves around it.

REMEMBER THIS, TOO, SAYS CARL D. LANE

Let the navigator and the mariner never forget a basic truth, unalterable by human emotions, weather conditions, or anything else, short of an explosion of the universe:

The Compass Never Lies

Have a good compass, properly adjusted for deviation; take care of it; and from that moment on

Trust Your Compass Over All Else

ALL SYSTEMS OF NAVIGATION ARE CONCERNED WITH THESE THREE MATTERS

Position

Direction

Distance

Out of sight of land the sailor feels safe.
It is the beach that worries him.
                              —Charles G. Davis

SEPTEMBER

Monday
8

1923—As the result of a navigational error, seven U.S. Navy destroyers—*Delphy, S.P. Lee, Fuller, Chauncey, Woodbury, Nicholas,* and *Young*—ran ashore in a fog, one after the other, at Point Honda, California.

Tuesday
9

1833—The first naval drydock built by the U.S. government was completed in Boston, Massachusetts.

Wednesday
10

1788—An English patent for the "Application of Paper to the Building of Houses, Bridges, Ships, Carriages, & etc." was issued to Charles Lewis Ducrest.

Thursday
11

She was radiant, she was an immortal beauty, that swaying, delicate clipper.
                              —John Masefield

Friday
12

1943—The *Terra Nova*, which had served as the base ship for Captain Robert Falcon Scott's ill-fated expedition to the South Pole, sank off Simiutak Island, Greenland.

Saturday
13

1856—Thomas F. McManus, New England fishing-schooner designer, creator of the racing fishermen *Esperanto* and *Henry Ford*, was born in Boston, Massachusetts.

Sunday
14

1851—James Fenimore Cooper, author of *The Pilot* and the *History of the Navy of the United States of America*, died.

BAROMETER READINGS

Published and broadcast barometer readings are taken at sea level. For every 10 feet above or below sea level, add or subtract .01 inch.

MOVEMENT MATTERS

The reading of the barometer at any given moment is not the key to weather prediction. Rather, it is the trend of a series of readings over a period of time.

Rapid rise—unsettled weather
Slow rise or a steady glass—fair weather
Alternate rise and fall—unsettled weather
Rapid fall—gale and rain

When sound travels far and wide,
A stormy day will like betide.

SOUND MATTERS, TOO

Sound travels better in air of higher humidity than low. A good hearing day—far-off sounds are easily heard—suggests that wet weather is on the way, whereas a bad hearing day suggests the onset of fair weather.

THOMAS B. MIDDLETON PROPOSES THE FIRST ONE-DESIGN CLASS

It is proposed to establish in Kingstown [Dun Laoghaire, Ireland] a class of sailing punts, with centreboards all built and rigged the same, so that an even harbour race may be had with a light rowing and generally useful boat. Gentlemen wishing to consider the proposition can have full particulars by applying to M 589, this office.

—*The Irish Times*

THREE TYPES OF BAROMETER

Mercury—a column of mercury in a vacuum tube is balanced by the pressure of the atmosphere.

Aneroid—the pressure of air is measured by the elasticity of a plate of metal.

Barograph—an aneroid barometer records its readings over time by a stylus operating on a moving sheet of paper.

COUNT THE STARS IN THE HALO

Out on the river there was a peaceful, motionless silence. The sky was streaky with clouds in the north and was open everywhere else. There were stars and a half-moon surrounded by a weak, misty halo. The proprietor stepped out of his office.

"How many stars in the halo?"

We counted three.

"It'll snow in three days," he said, and waved good-bye.

Three days later, just as he had promised, it snowed.   —from "Saturday Afternoon on the Eastern River," by P.H. Spectre

> *Two ships may be built to exactly the same design, but the one will behave like a pig at sea all her days, while the other never gives the slightest trouble to her crew.* —T.C. Lethbridge

SEPTEMBER

Monday
15
1912—Henry M. Plummer left New Bedford, Massachusetts, with his son and a cat aboard the catboat *Mascot* for a voyage down the East Coast to Florida. He later wrote about his cruise in *The Boy, Me, and the Cat*.

Tuesday
16
1926—The Gloucester schooner *Adventure*, last of the dory fishermen, was launched in Essex, Massachusetts. After many years in the Maine cruise-schooner fleet, she is now a sailing museum vessel in Gloucester.

Wednesday
17
1974—*Courageous* was successful in the 22nd defense of the America's Cup, defeating *Southern Cross* of the Royal Perth Yacht Club.

Thursday
18
1886—A proposal for a one-design sailing class, the first ever, was published in *The Irish Times*, leading, the following year, to the establishment of the Water Wag class.

Friday
19
1609—Henry Hudson, commander of the *Half Moon*, reluctantly concluded that the body of water he was exploring was a river (the Hudson), not a route to China.

Saturday
20
1967—The Cunard liner *Queen Elizabeth 2* was launched in Clydebank, Scotland.

Sunday
21
1957—The German auxiliary training bark *Pamir*, one of the last of the Cape Horners, sank with the loss of 80 lives during an Atlantic storm.

SEAMAN'S BILL OF FARE RECOMMENDED BY BRITAIN'S MERCHANT SHIPPING VICTUALLING SCALE COMMITTEE, 1892

Sunday
Breakfast—dry hash, soft bread
Dinner—sea-pie and plum duff
Supper—cold beef and pickles

Monday
Breakfast—Irish stew
Dinner—pea soup, pork, calavances
Supper—dry hash

Tuesday
Breakfast—rice and molasses
Dinner—salt beef, potatoes, plum duff
Supper—cold meat and pickles

Wednesday
Breakfast—porridge and molasses
Dinner—sea pie
Supper—potato stew

Thursday
Breakfast—Irish stew
Dinner—pea soup, pork, calavances
Supper—dry hash

Friday
Breakfast—dry hash
Dinner—preserved meat or salt fish and potatoes
Supper—twice laid of fish

Saturday
Breakfast—porridge and molasses
Dinner—salt beef, rice, and molasses
Supper—cold meat and pickles

In addition, daily
Breakfast—coffee, biscuit, butter, marmalade
Dinner—biscuits and switchel
Supper—tea, biscuits, butter, marmalade

AN UPPITY YANKEE DOODLE DANDY

Captain Pearson of the *Serapis*: "What ship is that?"

Captain John Paul Jones of the *Bonhomme Richard*: "Come a little closer and I will tell you."

Captain Pearson: "What are you laden with?"

Captain Jones: "Round, grape, and double-head shot."

SCALE OF PROVISIONS, SANCTIONED BY THE U.S. GOVERNMENT, ALLOWED SEAMEN ON BOARD THE AMERICAN SQUARE-RIGGED SHIP *A. J. FULLER*, 1897

Sunday
1 pound bread, 1½ pounds beef, ½ pound flour

Monday
1 pound bread, 1¼ pounds pork, 1⅛ pints peas

Tuesday
1 pound bread, 1½ pounds beef, ½ pound flour

Wednesday
1 pound bread, 1¼ pounds pork, 1⅛ pints peas

Thursday
1 pound bread, 1½ pounds beef, ½ pound flour

Friday
1 pound bread, 1¼ pounds pork, 1⅛ pints peas

Saturday
1 pound bread, ½ pounds beef

In addition, on each day seamen were provided with ⅛ ounce tea, ½ ounce coffee, 2 ounces sugar, 3 quarts water, and an issue of lime and lemon juice and sugar.

HOW TO BECOME AN ARISTOCRAT

Some time after the battle, Captain Pearson of the *Serapis* was knighted by King George. On hearing of it, John Paul Jones was reported to have said, "He deserves it; and if I fall in with him again, I'll make him a lord."

Monday

22   AUTUMNAL EQUINOX

1846—The *Great Western*, largest steamship of her time and the first vessel to cross the Atlantic with a screw propeller, ran ashore in Dundrum Bay, near Belfast, Northern Ireland.

Tuesday

23

1779—The *Bonhomme Richard*, commanded by Captain John Paul Jones, engaged and captured the frigate HMS *Serapis* off Flamborough Head, England. Shortly afterward, the *Richard* sank from battle damage.

Wednesday

24

1960—The first nuclear-powered air-craft carrier, the USS *Enterprise*, was launched in Newport News, Virginia.

Thursday

25

1962—*Weatherly* was successful in the 18th defense of the America's Cup, defeating *Gretel* of the Royal Sydney Yacht Club.

Friday

26

1983—On a black day for the New York Yacht Club, *Liberty* lost the America's Cup to the challenger, *Australia II* of the Royal Perth Yacht Club, thus ending the longest winning streak in sporting history (1851-1983).

Saturday

27

When men come to like a sea life, they are not fit to live on land.
—Dr. Samuel Johnson

Sunday

28

1066—A fleet of ships, commanded by William of Normandy, later known as William the Conqueror, crossed the English Channel and landed near Pevensey on the coast of Sussex, England.

TWO TYPES OF TOBACCO USED AT SEA DURING THE AGE OF SAIL

- That which was smoked
- That which was chewed

By far the preference among the crew was pipe smoking when it was permitted and chewing when it was not. Cigars were favored by the officers, with the pipe running a close second. In the last days of sail, cigarettes, almost always hand rolled, gained a hold on all classes of sailors. Given the difficulties of keeping specialized varieties on hand, the same tobacco was often used for pipes, cigarettes, and chewing. This was almost always "plug" tobacco, sometimes pressed cake, and was personally prepared by the user and wrapped in canvas. The chewer would simply cut off a piece of appropriate size with his rigging knife. The smoker would cut the plug or cake into thin slices and rub it out between the palms of his hands—coarse flakes for the pipe, fine flakes for cigarettes.

HOW PLUG TOBACCO WAS MADE

Tobacco leaves were soaked in honey, molasses, or other flavored syrup. Holes were drilled into a baulk of wood—hickory was preferred, but other species served in a pinch—and the sodden tobacco was forced into them (hence the word plug). Once the tobacco had cured, the plug was pulled from the hole and wrapped in canvas, ready for use.

A GOOD ALL-AROUND SEAGOING PIPE TOBACCO BLEND

Burley, 72 percent
Virginia, 25 percent
Latakia, 3 percent

To prevent the tobacco from burning too rapidly in windy conditions at sea, the cut should be coarse—cube, or moderately thick flake. Sliced-plug or pressed-cake pipe tobacco should not be rubbed out too much.

THE FINEST ERSATZ TOBACCO, ACCORDING TO REX CLEMENTS

Tobacco never tastes so good as in the salt air on ship-board, and is almost a necessity of existence in a hard-case "lime-juicer." A pipe of tobacco has often to serve in place of a meal and, rammed well down and glowing red in the bowl of a short clay, makes the cheeriest of companions in the long night watches. [Near the end of the voyage,] we felt the loss of it very keenly; the last few plugs changed hands at fancy prices, and when they were all gone our search for substitutes was exhaustive. Ropeyarns, whether manila or hemp, ravelled out, were tried and found very hot and heady; tea-leaves had their votaries, and some hardy spirits experimented with some of the green weed that decorated our waterline, dried in the sun. But the most popular smoke was a combination of ropeyarns, coffee-grounds and the bark off a pork-barrel, rubbed up small and mixed in equal quantities. If it had not the flavour of best Virginia it filled a place and we were thankful.

Monday
29
1951—A bottle with a message in it, the first of several hundred thrown into the ocean as a publicity stunt by the new magazine *Ships & Sailing*, was found ashore on Eleuthera Island, the Bahamas.

Tuesday
30
1976—The 73-foot proa *Crossbow II* set a new world speed record for sailing vessels of 31.8 knots off Portland Harbor, England.

Wednesday
1
1711—Alexander Selkirk, the model for Robinson Crusoe, rescued by the privateer Captain Woodes Rogers from Juan Fernandez Island, returned to England.

Thursday
2   ROSH HASHANAH
1962—The wreck of a Hanseatic cog, dating to the 14th century, was uncovered by a dredge working in the River Weser, Bremen, Germany.

Friday
3
1891—The fishing yawl *Resolute*, the first American beam trawler, was launched in Essex, Massachusetts.

Saturday
4
1901—*Columbia* was successful in the 11th defense of the America's Cup, defeating *Shamrock II* of the Royal Ulster Yacht Club.

Sunday
5
To all whose ambition it is to become good yachtsmen, I would by all means recommend them to commence their career in a small craft.   —Vanderdecken

COMPONENTS OF CANVAS

Warp—the threads running lengthwise
Weft—the threads running crosswise
Selvage—the finished edge

OLD METHOD OF REMOVING MILDEW FROM A COTTON SAIL

1. Spread out the sail in direct sunlight to dry.
2. Scrub the sail on both sides with fresh-water and soap.
3. Rub powdered whiting on remaining stains.
4. Leave the sail to dry and bleach in the sun, turning periodically.

OLD METHOD OF BLEACHING OUT A DISCOLORED COTTON SAIL

1. Lay out the sail and scrub both sides with seawater and saltwater soap.
2. Allow it to dry in the sun.
3. Sprinkle the sail on both sides with powdered whiting dissolved in seawater—the solution should look like milk.
4. Leave the sail to dry and bleach in the sun, turning it periodically.

TO TEST COTTON CANVAS FOR DETERIORATION

Bore a sample with a fid. If the threads are in poor condition, they will break easily.

PROTECTING STORED SAILS AND CUSHIONS FROM VERMIN

Rats and mice love to chew up stored canvas products during winter layup. They do this not because they are hungry, but because they are looking for material for their nests. Distract them with a stack of newspapers left out in the open near the sails and cushions; they will usually take the paper because it is easier to shred.

ROUGH FORMULA FOR FIGURING THE AREA OF SAIL REQUIRED TO DRIVE A BOAT WITH A DISPLACEMENT HULL

100 square feet of sail for every ton of displacement

TO MEASURE THE AREA OF A TRIANGULAR SAIL

Drop a vertical line from any corner to the opposite side. The length of the opposite side multiplied by half the vertical equals sail area.

TO MEASURE THE AREA OF A GAFF SAIL

Divide the sail into two triangles. Determine the area of each triangle using the method above. The sum of the areas of the two triangles equals the area of the sail.

THE EVOLUTION OF SAIL REDUCTION

1. Bonnet laced to the foot of the sail, which could be removed as the wind increased.
2. Reefing points in the sail, allowing a tuck to be taken in it. More rows of reefing points, more tucks.
3. Splitting up the sail area—several small sails rather than one or two large sails—allowing sails to be furled progressively as the wind increased.

Nail to the mast her holy flag,
Set every threadbare sail,
And give her to the god of storms,
The lightning and the gale!
—from "Old Ironsides," Oliver Wendell Holmes

OCTOBER

Monday
6

1884—The Naval War College was
established in Newport, Rhode Island.

Tuesday
7

1894—Oliver Wendell Holmes,
author of the poem "Old Ironsides,"
which was instrumental in saving
the U.S. frigate *Constitution*, died
in Boston, Massachusetts.

Wednesday
8

1719—Joseph Russell, founder
of the largest American whaling
fleet and builder of the first
sperm-oil factory in New Bedford,
Massachusetts, was born.

Thursday
9

1833—In the worst marine accident on
the Connecticut River, both boilers of
the new steamboat *New England*
exploded, killing 17 passengers and
crew and scalding many more.

Friday
10

1913—President Woodrow Wilson
removed the last obstruction in the
Panama Canal.

Saturday
11 YOM KIPPUR

1982—The wreck of the *Mary Rose*,
sunk in The Solent off Portsmouth,
England, in 1545, was salvaged. It is
now preserved in a specially constructed
building in Portsmouth.

Sunday
12

1492—Rodrigo de Triana, a
seaman aboard the *Pinta*, one
of three vessels in Christopher
Columbus's squadron, sighted
land to the west at 2 a.m.

LONGEVITY OF A THUNDERSTORM DEPENDS ON WHICH COMES FIRST, GENERALLY SPEAKING

If the wind comes before the rain during a thunderstorm, the dirty weather will be over quickly.

If the rain precedes the wind, the thunderstorm presages a longer spell of dirty weather.

YOU HAVE TWO CHOICES, ACCORDING TO R.T. MCMULLEN

If it looks like blowing hard on shore, get in somewhere in good time or else give the land a very wide berth.

MEETING A THUNDERSTORM IN A SMALL SAILBOAT

Thunderstorms generally come and go quickly.

If you are underway and see a thundercloud rising, douse all sails and lash them securely.

If the mast is light enough, unstep it.

Anchor, if possible, with a long scope, but do not anchor on a lee shore unless there is no other option.

If the water is too deep to anchor, prepare to run under bare poles.

If directional control is required, run under a small jib.

If there is enough sea room, lie to a sea anchor.

If you don't have a sea anchor, use a bucket tied to a bow line, or a couple of spars lashed together.

If the wind before the rain
  Soon you may make sail again.
If the rain before the wind
  Shorten sail and halyards mind.
                    —old sailor's weather saying

BASIC PRECAUTIONS FOR SQUALLS AND HEAVY WEATHER OFFSHORE

Close tightly all portholes and other openings.

Cover hatches and skylights with heavy canvas fastened down securely.

Rig lifelines to assist anyone having to go forward to handle sails and ground tackle.

Secure all deck gear; be especially careful that the anchors are lashed down so they cannot go adrift.

Down below, stow all loose materials and gear; make sure locker doors and drawers are shut tightly and securely against opening.

KNOW YOUR WEATHER, SAYS LORD BRASSEY

There is no situation in which knowledge is more truly power, none in which, under a due sense of the providential care of Heaven, it gives a nobler confidence to man, than at sea, amid the raging of a hurricane.

Hark, hark, I hear the North Wind roar,
See how he riots on the Shoar;
And with expanded Wings out-stretch,
Ruffels the Billows on the Beach.
                    —Charles Cotton

Monday
13 COLUMBUS DAY

1878—The Nantucket South Shoals Lightship parted her mooring cables during a fierce gale and eventually was driven 800 miles offshore, almost to Bermuda.

Tuesday
14

1882—William Atkin, naval architect and writer, was born in New York City.

Wednesday
15

A voyage is to many people like taking an emetic—they look at the medicine and wish it well over, and look at the sea and wish themselves *well over.*
—Robert Smith Surtees

Thursday
16

1928—The National 14, one of the most competitive British racing-dinghy classes, was granted international status by the International Yacht Racing Union.

Friday
17

1829—With the opening of the Deep Cut, the Chesapeake and Delaware Canal, connecting Delaware and Chesapeake Bays, was ready for traffic.

Saturday
18

1849—William Matson, founder of the Matson Line of San Francisco, was born in Lysekil, Sweden.

Sunday
19

And than saynt Brandon badde the shypmen to wynde up the sayle, and forth they sayled in Goddes name.
—The Voyage of Saynt Brandon, anon.

CHARACTERISTICS OF THE IDEAL COMBINATION ROWING-AND-SAILING BOAT

Partly decked (forward, aft, and side decks)

High coaming around the cockpit

As low a centerboard trunk as possible

No shifting ballast unless absolutely necessary

Low gunwales at the rowing station

Built-in flotation

A simple sailing rig that can be raised and struck quickly

No standing rigging

Simple running rigging

Spars that can be stowed in the boat

TRADITIONAL WATERCRAFT, HANDS DOWN, ACCORDING TO R.D. "PETE" CULLER

Having worked with everything from cheap skiffs up through yachts plain and fancy, and Uncle Sam's best in wood, I have long ago come to the conclusion that the traditional craft is by far the most economical and useful in the end, and the most pleasing to the eye.

NATHANIEL HOLMES BISHOP III

Nathaniel Holmes Bishop III was one of the pioneers in the use of very small craft for recreational adventure. Born in Medford, Massachusetts, in 1838, he hiked across the southern portion of South America when he was 17 years old and published a book about the experience (*The Pampas and Andes: A Thousand Mile Walk Across South America*, 1869). Bishop later moved to New Jersey and became a cranberry farmer. In 1874-75, after becoming active in the sport of canoeing, he voyaged along inland and coastal waters from Quebec to Florida in two small craft: the first was an 18-foot lapstrake sailing and paddling canoe, which at 300 pounds proved to be too heavy; the second was a 58-pound paper canoe built by Elisha Waters and Sons of Troy, New York. Shortly afterward, Bishop had a 12-foot Barnegat sneakbox specially constructed and then voyaged in her from Pittsburgh, Pennsylvania, to Florida via the Ohio and Mississippi Rivers and the Gulf Coast. His two books on these voyages—*The Voyage of the Paper Canoe* (1878) and *Four Months in a Sneakbox* (1879)—were extremely popular in the late 19th century and did much to advance the use of both paper boats and Barnegat sneakboxes, as well as to inspire others to undertake long voyages in small craft. Nathaniel Bishop was one of the founders of the American Canoe Association in 1880 and the first secretary of that organization. He died in 1902.

NATHANIEL HOLMES BISHOP III ESPIES THE PERFECT SMALL BOAT

To find such a boat—one that possessed many desirable points in a small hull—had been with me a study of years. I commenced to search for it in my boyhood—twenty-five years ago; and though I have carefully examined numerous small boats while travelling in seven foreign countries, and have studied the models of miniature craft in museums, and at exhibitions of marine architecture, I failed to discover the object of my desire, until, on the sea-shore of New Jersey, I saw for the first time what is known among gunners as the Barnegat Sneak-box.

Barnegat sneak box

Monday
20
1817—The first showboat, or floating theater, a converted Mississippi River keelboat, departed Nashville, Tennessee, for performances along the Cumberland, Ohio, and Mississippi Rivers.

Tuesday
21
1874—Nathaniel Holmes Bishop III began his voyage in the paper canoe *Maria Theresa* from Troy, New York, to Cedar Key, Florida. He wrote of his experiences in *The Voyage of the Paper Canoe*.

Wednesday
22
1707—Four ships of the Royal Navy ran ashore on the Scilly Isles off the coast of Cornwall, England, with the loss of almost 2,000 lives.

Thursday
23
1988—The *Pride of Baltimore II*, a reproduction of a Baltimore clipper built to her namesake, which was lost at sea in 1986, was commissioned in Baltimore, Maryland.

Friday
24
1921—The Lunenburg schooner *Bluenose* won the second International Fishermen's Race, defeating the Gloucester schooner *Elsie* in two straight matches.

Saturday
25
1861—The keel of the USS *Monitor* was laid.

Sunday
26
1788—HMS *Bounty* arrived in Tahiti to take on a cargo of breadfruit trees.

PERTINENT EXTRACTS FROM THE *CONDITIONS OF THE DEED OF GIFT FOR THE INTERNATIONAL FISHERMEN'S TROPHY*

The only vessels which can compete for the Trophy shall be bona fide fishing vessels, which have been engaged in commercial deep sea fishing for at least one season previous to the race.

The Captain and Crew of each competing vessel shall be bona fide fishermen, actively engaged in deep sea fishing.

All competing vessels shall be propelled by sails only.

The Sails used in racing shall be made of the ordinary commercial duck of the same weight and texture as generally used in this class of vessel and shall have been used at least one season in fishing.

LAYING HER UP FOR A WINTER SALE

If you expect to offer your boat for sale during the winter, be extra careful when you lay her up in the fall. Repaint and varnish as much as you can, and make sure the boat is neat and clean inside and out. Be especially sure to clean out the lockers and storage compartments. Polish the brass, wash the windows, clean any grease and oil off the engine, go over the galley with a fine-toothed comb, and sweep the cabin sole.

TO PROTECT BRASS DURING WINTER STORAGE

Polish the brass when the boat is hauled, then smear it with Vaseline or light machine oil, or spray it with WD-40.

WHEN HAULING FOR THE WINTER, TOUCH HER UP IMMEDIATELY

If there are any breaks in the surface coatings, spot paint or varnish to prevent weathering of the wood during the winter. In the spring, feather the edges of these spots with sandpaper before painting or varnishing the entire surface.

THREE TYPES OF WINTER STORAGE

Wet—in the water, in which case the superstructure and deck usually are covered with a tarpaulin over a temporary frame

Dry—on land, wrapped in a tarpaulin or under a temporary frame covered with a tarpaulin

Inside—in a shed or barn

Wet storage assumes the harbor is ice-free, or a bubbler system is used to prevent ice from forming alongside the hull.

Poppets and braces used to support a boat in dry storage should be carefully positioned, keeping in mind the likely heaving of the ground from frost.

For outside storage, the tarpaulin cover should be adequately pitched to allow snow and ice to slide off, and the framework supporting it should be strong enough to hold the weight of any snow and ice that does not.

Boats stored inside should be covered with a loose tarpaulin to keep off dust and dirt.

Whichever method is chosen, be sure the inside of the boat is well ventilated; otherwise, condensation will form and ruin the interior. Remove sails, cushions, mattresses, pillows, blankets, life jackets, and other materials susceptible to dampness, mold, and mildew and store them in a dry, well-ventilated space.

Until you do it all yourself you cannot have any idea of the innumerable minutiae to be attended to in the proper care of a yacht.
—John "Rob Roy" MacGregor

OCT/NOV

Monday
27
1915—Ernest Shackleton and his crew abandoned their ship, the *Endurance*, which had been frozen in the ice of the Weddell Sea, Antarctica, since the previous January.

Tuesday
28
1951—The tanker *Auris*, first merchant ship powered by a gas turbine, got underway from Hebburn-on-Tyne, England, for Port Arthur, Texas, on her maiden voyage with her new power plant.

Wednesday
29
1888—A convention was signed guaranteeing passage through the Suez Canal of vessels, armed or not, from all nations, in peace or war, and exempting the canal from blockade under all circumstances.

Thursday
30
1900—With the sailing of the new steamer *American* from New York City, the American-Hawaiian Steamship Company began operations.

Friday
31 HALLOWEEN
1958—The uncompleted hull of the USS *Kentucky*, last U.S. Navy battleship to be laid down, was sold for scrap.

Saturday
1
1920—The Gloucester schooner *Esperanto* won the first International Fishermen's Race series, defeating the Lunenburger *Delawana* in two straight matches.

Sunday
2
1867—John MacGregor completed the manuscript of *The Voyage Alone in the Yawl Rob Roy*, one of the most notable small-craft cruising stories in the English language.

NEW YORK'S WEDDING OF THE WATERS, CELEBRATING THE OPENING OF THE ERIE CANAL, FROM A CONTEMPORARY DESCRIPTION

The Aquatic display transcended all anticipations, twenty-nine steamboats, gorgeously dressed, with barges, ships, pilot-boats, canal-boats, and the boats of the Whitehall firemen, conveying thousands of ladies and gentlemen, presented a scene which can not be described. Add to this, the reflections which arise from the beauty and extent of our Bay—the unusual calmness and mildness of the day—the splendid manner in which all the shipping in the harbor were dressed, and the movement of the whole flotilla. Regulated by previously arranged signals, the fleet were thrown at pleasure, into squadrons or lines, into curves or circles. The whole appeared to move as by magic.

HERE'S WHY EVERYONE WAS SO HAPPY

Before the opening of the Erie Canal, the tariff for shipping a barrel of flour by wagon from Rochester to Albany, New York, was $3.00. After the Wedding of the Waters, the cost by canal boat was 75 cents.

THROWING A HEAVING LINE

1. Weight one end of the line with a monkey's fist or some other throwing weight.
2. Coil half the line, with the un-weighted end, into large bights.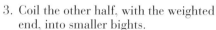

3. Coil the other half, with the weighted end, into smaller bights.
4. Hold the large-bight coil loosely in your nonthrowing hand.
5. Hold the small-bight coil tightly in your throwing hand.
6. Swing the throwing coil back and forth a few times to gain momentum.
7. Heave the throwing coil underhand, at the same time letting the large-bight coil run out as required.
8. Don't forget to hang on to your end of the line!

FLAKING DOWN A LINE SO IT WILL PAY OUT QUICKLY WITHOUT TANGLES OR SNARLS

1. Lay out the line on deck in a series of parallel, back-and-forth loops.
2. If deck space is limited, lay out as many loops as possible, then lay an additional layer of loops on top of, *and at right angles to*, the first layer.
3. If more than one layer of loops is used, keep in mind that the line must pay out from the top layer down.

TO REMOVE THE KINKS IN A FIBER ROPE

1. Coil the rope against the lay—i.e., left-handed for right-laid rope.
2. Pull the lower end up through the center of the coil, and then re-coil it with the lay—i.e., right-handed for right-laid rope.
3. If the rope is severely kinked, repeat the procedure.

Alternatively, stream the rope over the stern while underway until the kinks are worked out.

It would be difficult to describe the subtle brotherhood of men that was here established on the seas. —Stephen Crane

NOVEMBER

Monday

3

1913—The fishing schooner *Annie M. Parker*, abandoned by her crew two days earlier after striking a shoal, was found sailing herself east of Nantucket by the British steamer *Astrakhan*.

Tuesday

4 ELECTION DAY

Dr. Johnson said the pleasure of going to sea was getting to shore again; certainly the pleasure of a storm is getting into smooth water again.
          —Sir Edward Sullivan

Wednesday

5

1858—Stock went on sale to raise capital for the construction of a canal, the Suez, connecting the Mediterranean and Red Seas.

Thursday

6

1756—Commodore Richard Dale, naval hero of the American Revolutionary War and second in command aboard John Paul Jones's *Bonhomme Richard*, was born near Norfolk, Virginia.

Friday

7

1825—A symbolic "Wedding of the Waters" ceremony was held in New York Harbor to celebrate the opening of the Erie Canal, which provided cheap transportation between the eastern seaboard and the Midwest.

Saturday

8

1929—The Gloucester fishing schooner *Arethusa*, famous for her prodigious career as a rumrunner under Captain Bill "The Real McCoy" McCoy, struck a ledge off Halifax, Nova Scotia, and sank.

Sunday

9

1913—During a vicious three-day storm that began on this date, a total of 19 vessels were wrecked on the Great Lakes.

THE TERRORS OF LIGHTHOUSE CONSTRUCTION, IN THIS CASE THE SKERRYVORE, OFF THE WEST COAST OF SCOTLAND, IN THE LATE 1830S, ACCORDING TO ROBERT STEVENSON, CHIEF ENGINEER

For miles around nothing could be seen but white foaming breakers, and nothing heard but howling winds and lashing waves.... Our slumbers were at times fearfully interrupted by the sudden pouring of the sea over the roof, the rocking of the house on its pillars, and the spurting of water through the seams of the doors and windows.... On two occasions in particular, those sensations were so vivid as to cause almost every one to spring out of bed; and some of the men fled from the barrack by a temporary gangway to the more stable, but less comfortable, shelter afforded by the bare walls of the lighthouse tower, then unfinished, where they spent the remainder of the night in darkness, wet, and cold.

THE DIFFERENCE BETWEEN FLASHING AND OCCULTING LIGHTS

Flashing light—the period of light is shorter than the period of dark.

Occulting light—the period of light is equal to or longer than the period of dark.

WHITEWASH FOR PAINTING A LIGHT-HOUSE, ACCORDING TO A LATE-18TH-CENTURY FORMULA

Mortar mixed with hair, diluted sufficiently for application with a brush. For tenacity and to resist moisture, add one quart of new milk to each bucket of whitewash.

There's a sweet little cherub that sits up aloft

That looks out for the life of poor Jack.

—from an old song

INVENTORY OF EQUIPMENT AND SUPPLIES RECEIVED AT THE WATCH HILL, RHODE ISLAND, LIGHTHOUSE IN 1813, ACCORDING TO JONATHAN NASH, THE KEEPER

3 lamps	12 wick sticks	1 pound solder
1 stove	2 paint brushes	1 lantern canister
1 bucket	6 pounds paint	1 torch
5 wooden cisterns	4 quarts paint oil	2 tube cleaners
5 tin butts	13½ gross wicks	2 tin pans
2 spare lamps	14 dozen tube glasses	1 file
2 spare illumination glasses	1½ buff skins	1 pair pincers
5 wooden trivets	2 pairs shears	1 oil measure
2 wick boxes	13 yards cotton cloth	1 diamond
12 panes of glass	50 bushels charcoal	2 flanner trainers
15 pounds of putty	1 cord walnut wood	18 or thereabout bushels
1 lantern bin	1 jug	sea coal
2 gallons spirits of turpentine	1 tub	1 eclipser with apparatus
38 pounds whiting	1 soldering iron	for keeping in motion
	7 pounds rosin	

As far as yachting is concerned, there is not a
blasted thing here as good as it used to be.
                                    —L. Francis Herreshoff

NOVEMBER

Monday
10

1879—A convention was held at the Astor
House in New York City among several
eastern yacht clubs to develop plans for
a national yacht-racing association.

Tuesday
11 VETERAN'S DAY

1890—L. Francis Herreshoff, yacht
designer and author of such classics as
The Common Sense of Yacht Design
and *The Compleat Cruiser*, was born
in Rhode Island.

Wednesday
12

*It is nearly always the cautious sailor
and not the reckless one who succeeds
in sailing his little vessel to distant
shores.*   —E.F. Knight

Thursday
13

1970—A tropical cyclone with winds of
120 mph and a huge tidal wave struck
the Ganges River delta in Bangladesh,
causing the loss of hundreds of thousands of lives.

Friday
14

1909—Joshua Slocum, the first person to
circumnavigate the globe singlehanded,
was declared legally dead after presum-
ably being lost at sea. (This is the date
on which he last set sail.)

Saturday
15

1860—A new lighthouse was placed in
operation at Minot's Ledge, Massachusetts.
The original light had been swept away in
a northeast gale in 1851.

Sunday
16

1841—A patent was issued to
Napoleon E. Guerin of New York
City for the first cork-filled life pre-
server, a waistcoat or vest containing pockets of granulated cork.

MEMORABLE POEMS OF THE SEA

Annabel Lee, by Edgar Allan Poe ("It was many and many a year ago, In a kingdom by the sea....")

Crossing the Bar, by Alfred Lord Tennyson ("Sunset and evening star, And one clear call for me!...")

Drake's Drum, by Sir Henry Newbolt ("Drake he's in his hammock an' a thousand mile away....")

L'Envoi, by Rudyard Kipling ("There's a whisper down the field where the year has shot her yield, And the ricks stand gray to the sun....")

My Lost Youth, by Henry Wadsworth Longfellow ("Often I think of the beautiful town, That is seated by the sea....")

The Ocean, by Lord Byron ("There is a pleasure in the pathless woods, There is a rapture on the lonely shore....")

Off Riviere du Loup, by Duncan Campbell Scott ("O ship incoming from the sea....")

Old Ironsides, by Oliver Wendell Holmes ("Ay, tear her tattered ensign down!...")

Over the Sea to Skye, by Robert Louis Stevenson ("Sing me a song of a lad that is gone....")

Psalm 107, the Holy Bible ("They that go down to the sea in ships....")

The Rime of the Ancient Mariner, by Samuel Taylor Coleridge ("It is an ancient Mariner, And he stoppeth one of three....")

Rowers' Chant, by T. Sturge Moore ("Row till the land dip 'neath The sea from view....")

The Schipman, by Geoffrey Chaucer ("A schipman was ther, wonyng fer by weste....")

A Sea Dirge, by William Shakespeare ("Full fathom five thy father lies....")

Sea-Fever, by John Masefield ("I must down to the seas again, to the lonely sea and the sky....")

The Ship, by William Wordsworth ("Where lies the Land to which yon Ship must go?...")

Stowaway, by Bill Adams ("I crossed the gangway in the winter's raining, Late in the night, when it was dreary dark....")

The Three Fishers, by Charles Kingsley ("Three fishers went sailing away to the West....")

RECENT BOOKS ON SMALL-CRAFT CRUISING WORTHY OF MORE THAN PASSING ATTENTION

Princess—New York, by Joe Richards, 1956

Once Is Enough, by Miles Smeeton, 1959

The Boy, Me, and the Cat, by Henry M. Plummer, 1961

Tinkerbelle, by Robert Manry, 1965

Between Wind and Water, by Gerald Warner Brace, 1966

Gipsy Moth Circles the World, by Sir Francis Chichester, 1967

The Thousand Dollar Yacht, by Anthony Bailey, 1968

My Lively Lady, by Sir Alec Rose, 1969

The Strange Last Voyage of Donald Crowhurst, by Nicholas Tomalin and Ron Hall, 1970

A World of My Own, by Robin Knox-Johnston, 1970

Drifting, by Stephen Jones, 1971

I will go back to the great sweet mother,
Mother and lover of men, the sea.
—Algernon Charles Swinburne

NOVEMBER

Monday
17

1976—A 60-foot, serpentlike *Morgawr*—
Cornish for sea giant—was observed swim-
ming along the shore near Falmouth,
Cornwall, England.

Tuesday
18

1860—The clipper ship *Andrew Jackson*
arrived in New York at the end of a record
passage for commercial sailing vessels of
15 days from Liverpool, England.

Wednesday
19

The sailor out of water is, indeed,
as wretched an animal as the fish
out of water. —Henry Fielding

Thursday
20

1808—William Hackett, builder of
many of the greatest American ships
of the late 18th century, including the
naval frigates *Alliance* and *Essex*,
died in Salisbury, Massachusetts.

Friday
21

1908—Murray G. Peterson, yacht
designer, creator of the Coaster
cruising schooners, was born in
Cape Elizabeth, Maine.

Saturday
22

1916—Jack London—hobo,
socialist, war correspondent,
author of *The Sea Wolf*—died
near Santa Rosa, California.

Sunday
23

1857—The *Adriatic*, largest wooden
steamship built for the transatlantic
trade, embarked on her maiden voyage, her only one before being laid up,
from England to the United States.

Down on your knees, boys, holystone the
*   decks,*
Rub 'em down, scrub 'em down, stiffen out
*   your necks.* —Charles Keeler

THE RELIGIOUS DOCTRINE OF HOLYSTONING THE DECKS

Holystones, also known as ecclesiastical bricks, are used to clean and smooth wooden decks. Legend has it that at one time Britain's Royal Navy did the job with stone fragments from the ruined St. Nicholas Church in Great Yarmouth, England—hence the name.

Holystoning produces a handsome, snow-white surface on pine decks, but the technique wears away the wood, so too much of it, too often, eventually makes the deck too thin and ruins it structurally.

The larger stones, used for open spaces, are called "bibles."

The smaller ones, for getting into corners and working along the edges of the deck furniture and the rails, are called "prayer books."

The actual act of holystoning, wherein the sailors get down on their hands and knees with the stones, is known as "praying."

"Our knees became sore from constant praying," wrote Felix Riesenberg, a hand on the American full-rigged ship *A.J. Fuller* at the turn of the 20th century, "and the skin on our hands was worn down thin. To overcome the hardness of the deck, we rigged up pieces of board to which three cleats were nailed and a strip of old canvas stretched over them. This afforded a yielding cushion to kneel on and kept our legs out of the water swishing about with the rolling of the ship."

TO WHITEN DECKS

1. Mix 1 pound oxalic acid with 1 gallon fresh water.
2. Apply the solution with a mop, taking care not to get it on nearby paintwork.
3. Wash off with fresh water immediately.

TO REMOVE A RUST STAIN FROM A DECK

1. Make a solution of 1 part muriatic acid and 3 parts fresh water.
2. Brush it over the stain.
   Allow to stand for a few hours, then rinse with clean, fresh water.

WASHING THE PAINTWORK ABOARD THE SQUARE-RIGGED SHIP *A.J. FULLER*, 1897, ACCORDING TO FELIX RIESENBERG

We were not allowed the bucket of classic "sewgee" of the steamship sailor, a mixture of caustic soda, soft soap and water, but were provided with nothing but a small tin of brick dust and a rag of burlap; a rope-handled deck bucket and a small swab completed the outfit. Add to this formula an abundance of "elbow grease," and skithers of tropic rain, and you get paintwork polished smooth and white as ivory.

MODERN "SOOGEE," THE TRADITIONAL EXTERIOR WASHDOWN SOLUTION

Add 1 cup of detergent and 1 cup of bleach to a pail of fresh, hot water. Dip a stiff brush in the soogee and wash down. Clean up with a cotton mop, then flush with cold water.

Six days shalt thou labor and do all that thou
*   art able,*
And on the seventh holystone the deck and
*   scrape the cable.* —anon.

Monday
24
1922—Robert Erskine Childers,
member of the Irish Republican
Army and author of *The Riddle of
the Sands*, was executed in Dublin,
Ireland, by the Irish Free State.

Tuesday
25
1775—The Continental Congress
authorized the capture of any armed
vessel employed against the American
colonies, or any vessel carrying war
munitions to the British army or navy.

Wednesday
26
1703—A great storm struck the British
Isles, sinking or driving ashore hundreds
of ships. The Eddystone Light, in the
English Channel off Devon, was destroyed.

Thursday
27   THANKSGIVING
1926—The knockabout *Helen B.
Thomas*, the first Gloucester fishing
schooner rigged without a bowsprit,
was destroyed by fire while serving
as a Bermuda pilot boat.

Friday
28
1964—Yacht designer Samuel S.
Crocker, who had worked for many
years in John Alden's office before set-
ting up his own shop in Boston, died in
Beverly, Massachusetts, at the age of 74.

Saturday
29
*Let the most absent-minded of men be
plunged in his deepest reveries—stand
that man on his legs, set his feet going,
and he will infallibly lead you to water.*
            —Herman Melville

Sunday
30
1749—John Harrison, who was
to create the first accurate time-
piece for determining longitude
at sea, was awarded the Copley
Gold Medal for achievement.

Landing passengers at Natal, South Africa.

REQUIEM
by Robert Louis Stevenson

Under the wide and starry sky
Dig the grave and let me lie.
Glad did I live and gladly die,
And I laid me down with a will.

This be the verse you grave for me:
Here he lies where he longed to be;
Home is the sailor, home from sea,
And the hunter home from the hill.

NAME THAT TACKLE
A tackle is named according to the number of sheaves in its blocks—single, twofold or double, threefold or treble, fourfold or quadruple, etc.—and according to its use, such as whip, runner, luff, purchase, Spanish burton, etc.

A BLOCK-AND-TACKLE LEXICON
Block—a device used to change the direction of pull of a rope
   Single block—one sheave
   Double block—two sheaves
   Treble block—three sheaves
   Internal-bound block—a metal strop inside the shell
   External-bound block—a metal strop outside the shell
   Fiddle block—two sheaves, one above the other in the same shell
   Snatch block—fitted with a hinged clamp at the side to permit rope to be slipped over the sheave
   Patent block—one in which the sheave pin is surrounded by ball bearings or a roller bushing
   Tackle—blocks and rope arranged to multiply power
   Falls—the rope portion of a tackle
   Standing part—the part of the falls attached to a block
   Hauling part—the part of the falls that is hauled upon
   Reeve—to pass a rope through a block
   Two-block—to bring together two blocks of a tackle
   Overhaul—to separate two blocks of a tackle

A SAILOR'S CURSE
Big ropes and small blocks to ya!

—anon

LONGEVITY FOR A WOODEN-SHELL BLOCK
- Soak the shell well in linseed oil.
- Keep the sheave pin well lubricated.

HOISTING ON BOARD MONEY OR PLATE (FOR THOSE WHO HAVE THE GREAT, GOOD FORTUNE)
In hoisting on board money, plate, or other valuables, a buoy or buoy-rope, corresponding to the depth of water, ought always to be attached thereto, that in case of anything giving way, or the money or plate going to the bottom, there may be a ready means of recovery at hand. For boxes of treasure, strong nets, in place of slings, are most useful and most safe.   —from *The Kedge Anchor*, by William N. Brady (1876)

As it is written, the life of a man is a shadow, swiftly passing, and the days of his strength are less; but the sea shall endure in the might of youth to the wreck of the world. —Norman Duncan

DECEMBER

Monday
1

The sea is the great disturber. Nothing human can endure for long unchanged in its presence. —Filson Young

Tuesday
2

1865—Arthur Binney, yacht designer, whose most notable design was the America's Cup defense candidate *Pilgrim*, was born in Boston, Massachusetts.

Wednesday
3

1863—A fierce North Sea gale struck the English east coast fishing fleet; 165 smacksmen were lost from the port of Yarmouth alone.

Thursday
4

1894—Robert Louis Stevenson, author of *Kidnapped, An Inland Voyage*, and other books, died in Samoa, the South Pacific.

Friday
5

1775—For the first time, Commodore Esek Hopkins raised the "Don't Tread on Me" flag on the mainmast of the Continental Navy ship Alfred. The flag was decorated with 13 stripes without a union, and a rattlesnake.

Saturday
6

1830—The Secretary of the Navy ordered the establishment in Washington, DC, of a Depot of Charts and Instruments.

Sunday
7

1850—The *Stag Hound*, the first very sharp or extreme clipper and at the time the largest American merchant vessel, was launched in East Boston, Massachusetts, by Donald McKay.

Fogs, snowstorms, gales thick with clouds and rain—those are the enemies of good Landfalls.
—Joseph Conrad

SOMETIMES IT PAYS TO PRETEND YOU ARE A DOG, SAYS CARL D. LANE

Here on the coast of Maine [in the early 1940s] we have what is probably the strangest echo known. Coming in from Pemaquid toward Friendship in a thick o' fog, we run out our time to Cranberry Island, and to confirm the dead-reckoned fix, a man goes forward and howls like a dog. Almost immediately a dog howls or barks back. We're on course—for no matter when you howl at Mord Libby's dog on Cranberry Island he howls right back.

GEAR TO HAVE READY WHEN COMING ALONGSIDE A WHARF OR PIER

- Heaving lines
- Mooring lines
- Fenders
- Boathook

DOCKING, ANCHORING, OR PICKING UP A MOORING UNDER SAIL ALONE

Since a sailboat without wind in her sails will not sail, the principle is to sail almost to the destination and then to spill the wind by either letting the sheets fly or deliberately putting the vessel in irons, and then coast or "shoot" the rest of the way. The maneuver is successful if the vessel comes to a stop precisely at the destination. The experienced sailor determines when to begin shooting based on his knowledge of the momentum of his boat under various wind conditions and the state of the tidal current.

SIGNS OF A LANDFALL

A small cloud, seemingly fixed in position on the horizon, especially if other clouds around it are moving, may indicate an island or high hills or mountains on the mainland.

In cold climates, ice on or surrounding the land may throw a light-colored reflection on the underside of a uniform layer of clouds.

In tropical climates, a light green reflection on the underside of a layer of clouds may indicate the presence of a lagoon surrounded by islets.

Generally speaking, the color of the open ocean is of a dark shade because of the great depth. A lightening color may indicate shallowing water and the presence of land.

Land may be near if large numbers of birds appear. The more birds, the more likely land is nigh.

The direction of land can be roughly determined by the pattern of birds' flight. Generally speaking, birds fly toward the land at dusk and away from it at dawn.

The direction of land can be more accurately determined by studying the pattern of high-level airplane flight. Generally speaking, the higher the airplanes, the farther the land.

The presence and direction of an island can be roughly determined by studying the pattern of the swell. The swell will bend when it meets an island. Eddies are formed on the backside of an island—the "down-swell" side.

A high swell will produce heavy surf on land, especially if the shore is steep. The surf may be heard at a considerable distance, especially if atmospheric conditions are conducive to the carrying of sound.

Some land has a discernible odor, which will be strongest when the land is approached from downwind.

St. Helena

*A uniform course of honour and integrity
seldom fails of bringing a man to the goal
of fame at last.* —Admiral Lord Nelson

DECEMBER

Monday
8
1929—In the first commercial ship-
to-shore radiotelegraphic call, W.S.
Gifford, president of AT&T, rang up
Commodore Harold A. Cunningham,
at sea aboard the SS *Leviathan*.

Tuesday
9
1824—A crowd of 50,000 New Yorkers, one-third
of the city's population, turned out to watch the
pulling boat *American Star*, crewed by Whitehall
watermen, defeat the challenger *Dart*, from the
British frigate HMS *Hussar*, for a purse of $1,000.

Wednesday
10
1905—Relief Lightship 50, on
station at Nantucket Shoals, sank
in a gale. The crew was rescued
by the lighthouse tender *Azalea*.

Thursday
11
1866—The Great Ocean Race got underway from New York to Cowes, Isle of
Wight, England. The competitors were
the schooner-yachts *Henrietta*, *Fleetwing*,
and *Vesta*; the stake was $90,000.

Friday
12
*It is very common, amongst a certain class of
men, but nevertheless an absurd and dangerous fallacy; to suppose that because a vessel is
small, and of light draught, she can go any-
where without risk.* —R.T. McMullen

Saturday ◯
13
1907—The *Thomas W. Lawson*,
the only seven-masted schooner
ever built, was wrecked during a
storm in the Scilly Isles, off the
coast of Cornwall, England.

Sunday
14
1896—The Orient liner *Orotava*,
with water improperly distributed
in her ballast tanks, capsized and
sank while coaling at the Tilbury
Docks, London, England.

Stopped and riding to a drogue. Drifting slowly astern.

THE DAY FELIX RIESENBERG'S ASHES WERE SCATTERED ON THE SEA, ACCORDING TO CAPTAIN CROSS OF THE *CITY OF BALTIMORE*

The day was one which Felix would have loved—fine sailing weather, the sky partly cloudy, wind moderate S.E., and the sun flashing on the waves.

THE DANGERS OF BUCKING HEAVY HEAD SEAS IN A POWERBOAT

The hull can be structurally damaged by the pounding.

Heavy objects can come adrift and cause damage or instability before they are subdued.

The engine, transmission, shaft, or propeller can be damaged or broken by the alternating heavy load on the propeller when it is under water and no load, causing racing, when it is not.

HEAVING-TO IN A POWERBOAT

1. Head into the wind and sea.
2. Cut the engine to just enough rpm to provide steerageway but not headway.
3. Steer at an angle to the oncoming waves so the boat takes them on either bow.

THE LAW OF LARGENESS

The larger a vessel, the less engine power she requires in proportion to her size for a given speed.

THE SPEED-FUEL CONTINUUM, ACCORDING TO WESTON FARMER

There is no known form of locomotion that pays back such large fuel savings for cutting down speed as does a powered vessel.

***P**ower is a mighty valuable thing to have aboard a cruising boat.*
—William Washburn Nutting

THE ENGINEROOM TELEGRAPH

Also known as the annunciator, the engineroom telegraph consists of two devices, one on the bridge and one in the engineroom. Each has a circular dial with labels showing speeds ahead on the left and speeds astern on the right, and STOP at the top of the dial. The telegraphs at both stations have a handle and a pointer. The handle on the bridge controls the pointer in the engineroom, and the handle in the engineroom controls the pointer on the bridge. The officer on the bridge moves his handle to the desired speed; the motion causes a gong or bell to sound in the engineroom and the pointer on the engineer's telegraph dial to align with the label for the desired speed. The engineer will move his handle to the position indicated by the pointer; this will cause the pointer on the bridge telegraph to align with the label for the desired speed, thus indicating that the engineer understands the order.

Lying-to with engines stopped.

DECEMBER

Monday
15

1846—The Hakluyt Society—named after Richard Hakluyt, publisher of the *Principal Navigations, Voyages, and Discoveries of the English Nation*, was established to publish rare accounts of voyages and travels.

Tuesday
16

1773—Colonials dressed as Indians dumped tea from the British ships *Dartmouth*, *Eleanor*, and *Beaver* in a rebellious act that would become known as the Boston (Massachusetts) Tea Party.

Wednesday
17

1939—The German pocket battleship *Admiral Graf Spee* was scuttled off Montevideo, Uruguay, after an action with three British cruisers.

Thursday
18

1918—Washington Tarr, part owner of the Essex shipyard of Tarr & James, builders of such notable Gloucester fishing schooners as *Esperanto*, *Oriole*, *Thomas S. Gorton*, and *Arethusa*, died in Essex, Massachusetts.

Friday
19

1804—Marine artist Fitz Hugh Lane (né Nathaniel Rogers Lane), noted Luminist, was born in Gloucester, Massachusetts.

Saturday
20

1939—The ashes of Felix Riesenberg, deepwater sailor and author of *Under Sail*, *Cape Horn*, and other works, were scattered at sea off New York.

Sunday
21 WINTER SOLSTICE

1635—The keel of the *Sovereign of the Seas*, greatest and most ornate English warship of her time, was laid in Woolwich, England.

CHRISTMAS EVE, THE FIRTH OF FORTH, SCOTLAND, ACCORDING TO FILSON YOUNG

Orders came from the Commander-in-Chief that we were to sail at 7 p.m. on Christmas Eve; and as I was not likely to get much exercise for the next few days I took a solitary walk as far as Davidson's Mains and back. It was a day of clear, hard frost and full of the atmosphere of Christmas; and it was strange to leave the lights and the holly and the Christmas preparations of the shore and go out in the cold darkness of the night to spend our Christmas at sea.

THE DAWN OF THE DAY, ACCORDING TO FRANK BULLEN

On Christmas morning I mounted to the crow's nest at daybreak, and stood looking with never-failing awe at the daily marvel of the sunrise. Often and often have I felt choking for words to express the tumult of thoughts aroused by this sublime spectacle. Hanging there in cloudland, the tiny microcosm at one's feet forgotten, the grandeur of the celestial outlook is overwhelming. Many and many a time I have bowed my head and wept in pure reverence at the majesty manifested around me while the glory of the dawn increased and brightened, till with one exultant bound the sun appeared.

OFF THE CAPE OF GOOD HOPE, ACCORDING TO CAPTAIN JOSHUA SLOCUM

On Christmas, 1897, I came to the pitch of the cape. On this day the *Spray* was trying to stand on her head, and she gave me every reason to believe that she would accomplish the feat before night. She began very early in the morning to pitch and toss about in a most unusual manner, and I have to record that, while I was at the end of the bowsprit reefing the jib, she ducked me under water three times for a Christmas box. I got wet and did not like it a bit: never in any other sea was I put under more than once in the same short space of time, say three minutes. A large English steamer passing ran up the signal, "Wishing you a Merry Christmas." I think the captain was a humorist; his own ship was throwing her propeller out of water.

OFF CAPE HORN, TURN OF THE 20TH CENTURY, ACCORDING TO COLIN MCKAY

A Merry Christmas! It is at such times that the bitter ironies of life come home to a man—that the bitterness of the sea gets into the blood, the heart, the brain. I thought of the lucky landsmen, the owners of ships, sitting snug by their Yule-tide fires, with their wives and children around them and looked at our fo'castle—the abode of the men of the sea. A whooping sea had stove in the fo'castle door and a foot or so of water was surging back and forth over the floor ceaselessly. A grimy lamp, swinging under the carlins cast flickering gleams into the dungeon-like gloom of that reeking kennel. The ceiling and walls oozed water and everything was cold and cheerless like some horrid phantoms. In the bunks men with oilskins, boots, sou'wester, mitts, everything on them huddled under sodden blankets, their hairy and ghastly faces, their staring eyes, telling of sleepless days and nights, of relentless driving and bad and insufficient food, and as we sank into the numb lethargy that comes in lieu of sleep when a man is nigh worn out, the startling cry of "Ice, ice ahead, sir," rang along the decks . . . .

A hell of a Christmas Day, boys,
A hell of a Christmas Day,
For we are bound for the bloody Horn
Ten thousand miles away. —old sailor's ditty

DECEMBER

Monday
22

1938—A coelacanth, a fish thought
to have become extinct 70 million
years earlier, was caught off the
coast of South Africa.

Tuesday
23 CHANUKAH BEGINS

No man can understand the develop-
ment of the ship unless he realizes the
limitations of sail and the difficulties
with which the seamen of former ages
had to contend. —Alan Moore

Wednesday
24

1980—The Inland Navigational Rules Act, which
superseded the old Inland, Western Rivers, and
Great Lakes Rules, was enacted by the U.S.
Congress. The new rules almost completely unified
the old Inland and International Rules of the Road.

Thursday
25 CHRISTMAS

1878—W. Starling Burgess,
yacht designer, was born in
Boston, Massachusetts.

Friday
26

1945—Australia's first annual
Sydney-to-Hobart [Tasmania]
Race got underway.

Saturday
27

1904—J.M. Barrie's *Peter Pan*, in
which the archetypal pirate Captain
Hook played a pivotal role, was performed for the first time at the Duke
of York's Theatre, London, England.

Sunday
28

"I'm going to sea," said I.
"You can't go to sea, dear," she replied.
"I'm going to sea in the merchant ser-
vice," I retorted. —Bill Adams

GOOD-BYE, JACK, GOOD-BYE

Sailors were hard to kill thirty years ago [the 1890s], barring an accident, such as drowning or falling from aloft. They were a good deal like the jackass—they would grow so old that they would just wander away and die from old age.

—Arthur Mason

The ship is old, the grub is bad.
  Leave her, Johnny, leave her.
I'm getting thin, I'm growing
    sad;
  It's time for us to leave her.
The sails are furled, our work is
    done,
  Leave her, Johnny, leave her,
And now ashore we'll have some
    fun;
  It's time for us to leave her.

—old chanty

FIDDLER'S GREEN, AVALON, VALHALLA—ALL ROLLED INTO ONE PARADISE FOR SEAMEN—AS RELATED TO JOHN MASEFIELD BY A DANISH SAILOR

"When they have got to where the sun is, the red ball will swing open like a door, and Moby Dick, and all the whales, and all the ships will rush through it into an anchorage in Kingdom Come. It will be a calm piece of water, with land close aboard, where all the ships of the world will lie at anchor, tier upon tier, with the hands gathered forward, singing. They'll have no watches to stand, no ropes to coil, no mates to knock their heads in. Nothing will be to do except singing and beating on the bell. And all the poor sailors who went in patched rags, my son, they'll be all fine in white and gold. And ashore, among the palm-trees, there'll be fine inns for the seamen, where you and I, maybe, will meet again, and spin yarns, maybe, with no cause to stop until the bell goes."

NEW YEAR'S DAY
Children's song lyrics by Grace Rhys

I saw three ships come sailing by,
  Sailing by, sailing by,
I saw three ships come sailing by
  On New Year's Day in the morning.

And what do you think was in them then?
  In them then, in them then?
And what do you think was in them then,
  On New Year's Day in the morning?

Three pretty girls were in them then,
  In them then, in them then,
Three pretty girls were in them then,
  On New Year's Day in the morning.

And one could whistle and one could sing,
  And one could play on the violin,
Such joy there was at my wedding,
  On New Year's Day in the morning.

Most modern calendars mar the sweet simplicity of our lives by reminding us that each day that passes is the anniversary of some perfectly uninteresting event. —Oscar Wilde

DEC/JAN

Monday
29

1862—The Union ironclad *Monitor*, under tow from Fort Monroe, Virginia, to Charleston, South Carolina, sank in a heavy gale off Cape Hatteras.

Tuesday
30

1865—Rudyard Kipling, author of *Captains Courageous* and *The Seven Seas*, was born in Bombay, India.

Wednesday
31

1600—The British East India Company, one of the greatest maritime trading enterprises of its time, was founded.

Thursday
1   NEW YEAR'S DAY

1932—The first annual edition of *Reed's Nautical Almanac* was published. Edited by Captain O.M. Watts, it was initially called *Reed's Home Trade Nautical Almanac and Tide Tables*.

Friday
2

1892—Dennison J. Lawlor, naval architect, known for his fishing-schooner designs, among them the great *Harry L. Belden*, died in Chelsea, Massachusetts.

Saturday
3

1841—Herman Melville departed New Bedford, Massachusetts, on the whaler *Acushnet*. The ensuing voyage provided the background for Melville's novel *Moby-Dick*.

Sunday
4

For how like to life is the voyage of the great sailing ship? —Alan Villiers

1997

JANUARY

S	M	T	W	T	F	S
			1	2	3	4
5	6	7	8	9	10	11
12	13	14	15	16	17	18
19	20	21	22	23	24	25
26	27	28	29	30	31	

FEBRUARY

S	M	T	W	T	F	S
						1
2	3	4	5	6	7	8
9	10	11	12	13	14	15
16	17	18	19	20	21	22
23	24	25	26	27	28	

MARCH

S	M	T	W	T	F	S
						1
2	3	4	5	6	7	8
9	10	11	12	13	14	15
16	17	18	19	20	21	22
23	24	25	26	27	28	29
30	31					

APRIL

S	M	T	W	T	F	S
		1	2	3	4	5
6	7	8	9	10	11	12
13	14	15	16	17	18	19
20	21	22	23	24	25	26
27	28	29	30			

MAY

S	M	T	W	T	F	S
				1	2	3
4	5	6	7	8	9	10
11	12	13	14	15	16	17
18	19	20	21	22	23	24
25	26	27	28	29	30	31

JUNE

S	M	T	W	T	F	S
1	2	3	4	5	6	7
8	9	10	11	12	13	14
15	16	17	18	19	20	21
22	23	24	25	26	27	28
29	30					

JULY

S	M	T	W	T	F	S
		1	2	3	4	5
6	7	8	9	10	11	12
13	14	15	16	17	18	19
20	21	22	23	24	25	26
27	28	29	30	31		

AUGUST

S	M	T	W	T	F	S
					1	2
3	4	5	6	7	8	9
10	11	12	13	14	15	16
17	18	19	20	21	22	23
24	25	26	27	28	29	30
31						

SEPTEMBER

S	M	T	W	T	F	S
	1	2	3	4	5	6
7	8	9	10	11	12	13
14	15	16	17	18	19	20
21	22	23	24	25	26	27
28	29	30				

OCTOBER

S	M	T	W	T	F	S
			1	2	3	4
5	6	7	8	9	10	11
12	13	14	15	16	17	18
19	20	21	22	23	24	25
26	27	28	29	30	31	

NOVEMBER

S	M	T	W	T	F	S
						1
2	3	4	5	6	7	8
9	10	11	12	13	14	15
16	17	18	19	20	21	22
23	24	25	26	27	28	29
30						

DECEMBER

S	M	T	W	T	F	S
	1	2	3	4	5	6
7	8	9	10	11	12	13
14	15	16	17	18	19	20
21	22	23	24	25	26	27
28	29	30	31			

1996

JANUARY
S	M	T	W	T	F	S
	1	2	3	4	5	6
7	8	9	10	11	12	13
14	15	16	17	18	19	20
21	22	23	24	25	26	27
28	29	30	31			

FEBRUARY
S	M	T	W	T	F	S
				1	2	3
4	5	6	7	8	9	10
11	12	13	14	15	16	17
18	19	20	21	22	23	24
25	26	27	28	29		

MARCH
S	M	T	W	T	F	S
					1	2
3	4	5	6	7	8	9
10	11	12	13	14	15	16
17	18	19	20	21	22	23
24	25	26	27	28	29	30
31						

APRIL
S	M	T	W	T	F	S
	1	2	3	4	5	6
7	8	9	10	11	12	13
14	15	16	17	18	19	20
21	22	23	24	25	26	27
28	29	30				

MAY
S	M	T	W	T	F	S
			1	2	3	4
5	6	7	8	9	10	11
12	13	14	15	16	17	18
19	20	21	22	23	24	25
26	27	28	29	30	31	

JUNE
S	M	T	W	T	F	S
						1
2	3	4	5	6	7	8
9	10	11	12	13	14	15
16	17	18	19	20	21	22
23	24	25	26	27	28	29
30						

JULY
S	M	T	W	T	F	S
	1	2	3	4	5	6
7	8	9	10	11	12	13
14	15	16	17	18	19	20
21	22	23	24	25	26	27
28	29	30	31			

AUGUST
S	M	T	W	T	F	S
				1	2	3
4	5	6	7	8	9	10
11	12	13	14	15	16	17
18	19	20	21	22	23	24
25	26	27	28	29	30	31

SEPTEMBER
S	M	T	W	T	F	S
1	2	3	4	5	6	7
8	9	10	11	12	13	14
15	16	17	18	19	20	21
22	23	24	25	26	27	28
29	30					

OCTOBER
S	M	T	W	T	F	S
		1	2	3	4	5
6	7	8	9	10	11	12
13	14	15	16	17	18	19
20	21	22	23	24	25	26
27	28	29	30	31		

NOVEMBER
S	M	T	W	T	F	S
					1	2
3	4	5	6	7	8	9
10	11	12	13	14	15	16
17	18	19	20	21	22	23
24	25	26	27	28	29	30

DECEMBER
S	M	T	W	T	F	S
1	2	3	4	5	6	7
8	9	10	11	12	13	14
15	16	17	18	19	20	21
22	23	24	25	26	27	28
29	30	31				

1998

JANUARY
S	M	T	W	T	F	S
				1	2	3
4	5	6	7	8	9	10
11	12	13	14	15	16	17
18	19	20	21	22	23	24
25	26	27	28	29	30	31

FEBRUARY
S	M	T	W	T	F	S
1	2	3	4	5	6	7
8	9	10	11	12	13	14
15	16	17	18	19	20	21
22	23	24	25	26	27	28

MARCH
S	M	T	W	T	F	S
1	2	3	4	5	6	7
8	9	10	11	12	13	14
15	16	17	18	19	20	21
22	23	24	25	26	27	28
29	30	31				

APRIL
S	M	T	W	T	F	S
			1	2	3	4
5	6	7	8	9	10	11
12	13	14	15	16	17	18
19	20	21	22	23	24	25
26	27	28	29	30		

MAY
S	M	T	W	T	F	S
					1	2
3	4	5	6	7	8	9
10	11	12	13	14	15	16
17	18	19	20	21	22	23
24	25	26	27	28	29	30
31						

JUNE
S	M	T	W	T	F	S
	1	2	3	4	5	6
7	8	9	10	11	12	13
14	15	16	17	18	19	20
21	22	23	24	25	26	27
28	29	30				

JULY
S	M	T	W	T	F	S
			1	2	3	4
5	6	7	8	9	10	11
12	13	14	15	16	17	18
19	20	21	22	23	24	25
26	27	28	29	30	31	

AUGUST
S	M	T	W	T	F	S
						1
2	3	4	5	6	7	8
9	10	11	12	13	14	15
16	17	18	19	20	21	22
23	24	25	26	27	28	29
30	31					

SEPTEMBER
S	M	T	W	T	F	S
		1	2	3	4	5
6	7	8	9	10	11	12
13	14	15	16	17	18	19
20	21	22	23	24	25	26
27	28	29	30			

OCTOBER
S	M	T	W	T	F	S
				1	2	3
4	5	6	7	8	9	10
11	12	13	14	15	16	17
18	19	20	21	22	23	24
25	26	27	28	29	30	31

NOVEMBER
S	M	T	W	T	F	S
1	2	3	4	5	6	7
8	9	10	11	12	13	14
15	16	17	18	19	20	21
22	23	24	25	26	27	28
29	30					

DECEMBER
S	M	T	W	T	F	S
		1	2	3	4	5
6	7	8	9	10	11	12
13	14	15	16	17	18	19
20	21	22	23	24	25	26
27	28	29	30	31		

DON'T BE CAUGHT ABACK!
Next year has more dates and new facts

Each edition of *The Mariner's Book of Days* contains different information of interest and concern to the mariner, adding substance to an
encyclopedia of fact, legend, and lore. The unique reference value of
the material deserves a place on any bookshelf when the work of the
calendar is done. We invite you to ensure that you receive your next
copy. Send us your order for *The 1998 Mariner's Book of Days* today,
and receive it in plenty of time to plan the year ahead.

Please send _____ copies of *The 1998 Mariner's Book of Days* to:

Name_____

Address_____

_____

City/State/Zip_____

Price per copy is $12.95. Two or more copies are $11.00 each.
Please include $3.00 for shipping.
Maine residents please add 6% sales tax.

Mail your order to:
The WoodenBoat Store
P.O. Box 78, Naskeag Road
Brooklin, Maine 04616

Or Call Toll-Free 1-800-273-SHIP (7447)
8 A.M. – 6 P.M. EST, Monday through Friday.
VISA, Master Card, Discover are welcome.
FAX your credit card order to 207-359-8920.
E-mail your credit card order to: wbstore@woodenboat.com
Payment must be in U.S. funds, payable on a U.S. bank.

Discover WoodenBoat...
The unique magazine of wooden boats— past, present, and future

A publication of rare quality, *WoodenBoat* magazine combines magnificent graphics and color photography with editorial material that is rich, informative, and inspiring.

Each issue features practical and historical information on wooden boats built for speed, for sail, and for paddling at leisure. You'll receive expert advice on how to build, care for, and enjoy these wonderful boats—from birchbark canoes to four-masted schooners, from classic runabouts to the most powerful world-class racers.

You can get *WoodenBoat* now, just by completing the card below and mailing it to us today!

Or call: 1-800-877-5284

Subscribe to WoodenBoat!

☐ **YES!** Please start my subscription to *WoodenBoat* magazine for one year at only $27.

NO COST. NO OBLIGATION
If you are not delighted with your first issue, simply write "Cancel" on your bill, return it in the envelope provided and that's the end of the matter. The first issue is yours to keep.

SEND NO MONEY NOW. WE'LL BILL YOU LATER.

Name_____

Address_____

City_____

State/Zip_____

(In Canada, add $5. U.S. funds. Overseas, add $12, U.S. funds.) *WoodenBoat* is published six times a year. New subscriptions will start within 6–8 weeks.

A6BOD

BUSINESS REPLY MAIL
FIRST CLASS MAIL   PERMIT NO. 1   BROOKLIN, ME

POSTAGE WILL BE PAID BY ADDRESSEE

WoodenBoat

Subscription Department
P.O. Box 78, Naskeag Road
Brooklin, Maine 04616-9988